THE FRENCH COMMUNES IN THE MIDDLE AGES

Europe in the Middle Ages
Selected Studies

Volume 6

General Editor

RICHARD VAUGHAN
University of Hull

NORTH-HOLLAND PUBLISHING COMPANY – AMSTERDAM · NEW YORK · OXFORD

THE FRENCH COMMUNES
IN THE MIDDLE AGES

By

CHARLES PETIT-DUTAILLIS

Translated by
Joan Vickers

1978

NORTH-HOLLAND PUBLISHING COMPANY – AMSTERDAM · NEW YORK · OXFORD

Library of Congress Catalog Card Number: 76-29621
North-Holland ISBN: 0 7204 0550 5

Published by:
North-Holland Publishing Company – Amsterdam/New York/Oxford

Distributors for the U.S.A. and Canada:
Elsevier North-Holland, Inc.
52, Vanderbilt Avenue, New York, N.Y. 10017

Library of Congress Cataloging in Publication Data
Petit-Dutaillis, Charles Edmond, 1868–1947.
  The French communes in the Middle Ages.

  (Europe in the Middle Ages; v. 6)
  Translation of Les communes françaises.
  1. Municipal government--France--History. 2. Cities and towns--France--History. I. Title.
JS4821.P413   352'.008'0944   76-29621
ISBN 0-7204-0550-5

Printed in The Netherlands

293975

General Editor's preface

This is a translation of the first two-thirds of Charles Petit-Dutaillis' classic work which was published in French in 1947 in the series *L'évolution de l'humanité* with the title: *Les communes françaises. Caractères et évolution dès origines au XVIII*e *siècle.* The post-medieval section has been omitted as being of limited interest nowadays; the notes and bibliography because they have become largely out of date and are, in any case, available in the French edition. The aim has been to make available for the English-speaking student and general reader the only detailed and critical account of a fascinating and important historical phenomenon. The author discusses in considerable detail the medieval history of some twenty leading French towns, providing a factual framework rich in illustrative documentary material which retains almost all its value thirty years after it was written, in spite of changes in the attitudes and interpretations of historians.

The translator's text has been revised by myself; a few of the author's historiographical digressions have been omitted; the index is the translator's.

May 1976

Richard Vaughan
General Editor

Contents

**BOOK II   THE CLOSE OF THE MIDDLE AGES. CRISES.
                    DISAPPEARANCES. REVIVALS**

BOOK I FROM THE ORIGINS TO THE THIRTEENTH CENTURY

CHAPTER 1

Definition of the commune

1. Obscurity of current definitions

The history of urban liberties in the Middle Ages, which is one of the fields in which we can best appreciate our ancestors' efforts to organize justice and order, needs more to advance it than the slow publication of texts and of rigorous monographs. It is also important that the general concepts used in teaching this history and in presenting it to the public should be accurate. In fact, scholars often base their interpretation of fresh documentary evidence on general doctrines which they have accepted uncritically and which occasionally mislead them, as will be seen later. The provisional conclusions advanced in books by such eminent scholars as Luchaire and Pirenne need to be revised without too exaggerated a respect for their authors. Every scholar can be mistaken. Every scholar tends to overstress the importance of his theories; any excesses they contain are then accentuated by disciples more uncompromising than their master. The history of the communes in France and of the boroughs in England presents striking examples of contradictions, and of misunderstanding of texts, and has proved a rich source of confusion to minds already confused. I shall attempt, by referring to texts already published, to dispel some of the obscurities which distort the teaching of history as it concerns the French communes.

My main concern will be a problem of definition, and I shall begin by examining what right was conferred by the granting of a commune. The current reply to this question consists of incoherent explanations or sceptical denials which the texts do not warrant. It is in fact possible, for any given period, to give a short, precise definition of the commune, just as English scholars have succeeded in formulating the undoubtedly complex characteristics which distinguish the borough. But these

3

institutions evolved somewhat rapidly, and so they will require not one but several successive definitions.

An educated Frenchman whose knowledge of the Middle Ages derives from school history lessons, a reading of literature and some familiarity with monuments, knows more or less what is meant by an abbey, a knight, a vassal, or a serf. But the word 'commune' merely conjures up in his mind a vague picture of a belfry and the notion of a body of wealthy burgesses who have shaken off seigneurial rule, possess a law-court and magistrates, and form a militia. He thinks of Etienne Marcel, and when told that Paris was not a commune he is amazed because he draws no distinction between communes and other free towns. It is hard to see where he could have learned of this distinction. If he consults Littré, he will find that 'commune' means "under the feudal system the body of burgesses in a town or borough who have received a charter granting them the right to self-government" – a formula which does not cover all communes and is applicable to towns other than communes. If he goes to the standard manuals, including those written by qualified medievalists, he fares no better. One author gives a lengthy description of the commune without defining it; another states that communes are "towns which had political self-government and which have been styled collective seigneuries". The true definition is not given.

A similar confusion is apparent in works published around 1900 on French institutions, which are, naturally enough, the sources relied on by writers of popular history. The books which come nearest to the truth on this question are the great manuals on the history of French law, which are unfortunately not much used outside the law faculties. Jurists are meticulous about precise definitions, and their unfortunate tendency to split hairs and to shed light even in corners where none existed before, becomes a positive advantage when directed to a question like this. Even so, if we open Esmein's *Course*, edited by Génestal, we shall find that "The word commune has two meanings in the language of the Middle Ages"; "in its first broad meaning it denotes any town with a complete municipal organisation", etc., and "in its narrower meaning the word commune denotes the commune agreed on oath". This is "first and foremost a sworn association" which "usually coincides with the maximum grant of franchise". The true definition is here completely blurred. More recently Declareuil defined the commune as a "free town completely liberated from all seigneurial authority and itself constituted as a seigneury". Emile Chénon, who produced some conscientious and detailed studies on urban history, placed blind faith, as is evident from his conclusions, in statements advanced by scholars like Luchaire. In the teeth of textual evidence to the contrary, he states that every commune is characterized, first by the charter from the seigneur allowing the burgesses to run their own administration, secondly by the confirmation of the suzerain, and only thirdly by the oath of mutual aid sworn by the burgesses after the granting of the charters. This is putting the cart before the horse. Paul Viollet, the most learned of those jurists who produced a manual of French institutions, and certainly the one most familiar with the texts, follows the usual pattern when he admits that he is at a loss to know "what is the essential feature of a commune". He goes on to say: "For me, the idea of a commune was mainly the right of a considerable group of inhabitants to have proxies or personal representatives", but on the very next page he says that his definition applies to towns which were not called communes, such as Beaumont-en-Argonne and its daughter towns.

Sound monographs and interesting studies on the communes have been written by other scholars apart from jurists. It is surely appropriate to expound, first of all, the views of Arthur Giry, who was, at the close of the nineteenth century, acknowledged as having imparted new impetus and given fresh direction to research into municipal history in France. In a book he brought out together with André Réville, who wrote the work from notes supplied by Giry, to whom he then submitted them for revision, we read: "Historians are accustomed to separate towns into two clear-cut types; communes and *villes de bourgeoisie* (literally 'towns with burgesses').... This division is a pure convention. It does not date from the Middle Ages (*sic*) and in practice it would be difficult to distinguish the less free communes from the more independent of the *villes de bourgeoisie*".

However, several years previously, in 1890, Achille Luchaire had felt able to devote a whole book to the *Communes françaises*. It contains no definitive solution. He was struck by the undoubted confusions of medieval vocabulary and the complexity and incoherence of the charters; indeed this is the overriding impression conveyed to the reader. His only clear teaching on the character of the commune is what one might call his feudal and military theory, to which we shall return. It is for the most part accurate, but it fails to provide the technical definition we need.

More recent publications on the subject are those of Pirenne, Miss Lodge and Carl Stephenson. Pirenne, in an exposé often less lucid than it seems, asserts that "there is no need to establish any essential distinction between *villes de commune* and other towns.... They are basically similar in nature and they are all real communes". He goes on to state that "the only feature specific to communes *strictu sensu* is that they retained traces of their insurrectionary origin, just as if they all originated in an uprising".

In Volume Five of the *Cambridge medieval history*, published in 1926, Miss Lodge, who was commissioned to write the chapter 'The communal movement, especially in France', declares that it is impossible to draw a distinction between the French commune and the *ville de bourgeoisie*. In 1932, Carl Stephenson, in his laboriously constructed work entitled *Borough and town*, prefers to steer clear of a difficulty that he says does not exist. The term 'commune' for him, has no specific connotations, since all the characteristics of the commune are encountered in any *ville de franchises* to which this name is not applied. "Historically, the communes constituted no distinct group apart from other towns. Rightly to classify the municipalities of medieval Europe, we must ignore accidental titles and examine actual privileges."

Other scholars, by contrast, have given the word 'commune' an exact, unvarying meaning, which in my opinion is incorrect. Georges Espinas, a scholar most deeply versed in the documents appertaining to municipal history, published in 1943 three fat volumes of texts, each with an introduction by him. In his view, which I shall show was mistaken, the distinguishing marks of a commune were franchises of a specific type. For example, the act establishing the franchises of Noeux-les-Mines "certainly seems to have a communal significance", though it is not clear why. But Espinas goes further. He thinks he knows better than the men of the Middle Ages what a commune was and, rather oddly, denies the suzerain granting the charter the right to declare that he has no intention of creating a commune. In 1346 Eudes, count of Artois, and the Countess Jeanne, granted the town of Béthune a belfry, which was one of the outward marks of a commune, and they added: "And we make known that it is not our intent or desire that as a result of this concession made to the echevins, provosts, mayors and inhabitants of the said town, according to the tenor of these presents, a commune be granted or given them." M. Espinas is amazed. "They were playing on words a little (*sic*) since the town possessed an *échevinage* elected by co-optation, which in turn, in co-operation with the common people, elected a provost and two mayors. It follows that its constitution was certainly communal in type."

I hold firm to my belief that the jurists of the Middle Ages, when drawing up an act denying the right to a commune, knew perfectly well what they were about. It now remains to discover what meaning they gave the word 'commune' from one era to another.

2. The technical meaning of the word 'commune'

It must be stated at the outset that negative solutions have to be rejected and that the distinction between 'communes' and other *bonnes villes* (literally 'good towns') dates from the Middle Ages. The kings of France and the lords who granted communes gave the term a specific connotation. There is evidence as early as the twelfth century that communes were quashed, which doubtless implies that they were regarded as a privilege. Louis IX, in his ordinances on the accountability of towns, refers to communes and *bonnes villes* as if they were two quite distinct groups. Philip Augustus drew the same distinction. The fact that he was careful not to confuse the inhabitants "of his communes" with "his burgesses" and that he wrote "to all his dear mayors and sworn members of communes" shows that in fact the communes formed, in his domain and the territories over which he held undisputed sway, a clearly determined numerical group. Lastly, there is a decisive document which renders any further quotation unnecessary. After the considerable annexations to his kingdom at the beginning of the thirteenth century, and the submission of several barons and towns which no longer owed allegiance to the king of England, Philip Augustus had lists drawn up of vassals, fiefs and services, so as to have an organized, easily accessible catalogue of his rights and above all of his military resources. It was published under the title *Scripta de feodis*, from the various chancery registers dating from his reign. Some of these statistics are found in the *Registrum veterius*, written between 1204 and 1212. Of particular interest, on folio 6b and folios 7a and 7b are the lists of vassals, which must date from the years 1204–1206. These are first: *Archiepiscopi et episcopi qui sunt sub rege Francie*; then *Abbates regales*; then *Castellani*; then *Vavassores*; and finally *Communie*. This last list, written in the same hand as the preceding ones, ends the series of statistics found at the beginning of the register (in the present arrangement of the folios); after it come the charters of the communes. The enumeration of these includes thirty-nine towns or boroughs in the Ile-de-France, the Orleanais, Artois, the Vermandois, Normandy, Poitou, etc. They are towns of the royal domain or episcopal towns like Noyon and Beauvais, which the king assumes he can count on. Some of them were of considerable size, whereas others were small rural communities. Paris, Orléans, and many other large towns, which were in the royal domain or subject to the king's authority, do not appear in this official list of the king's communes. It follows that 'commune' must be a technical term.

I shall show in a later chapter that, although the meaning of the word did not remain constant throughout the Middle Ages, it was always used in a specialized manner. For example, in the fourteenth century, when the institution was on the decline, and the term describing it might well have become somewhat vague, the king refers to his "several other *bonnes villes* in our kingdom, in which there is no commune". On another occasion he declares: "The citizens, burgesses and inhabitants of our town of Mâcon ... form neither a corporate body nor a commune."

One way of arriving at the technical meaning of the word 'commune' is to try to collect all the examples of its use in eleventh- and twelfth-century texts, and then to extract a definition from this list. Such a method, which scholars – English scholars in particular – have sometimes used with great success, and which can produce new and surprising results, would still not take us far enough. That is not to say it would be unprofitable. We should discover that the word almost constantly relates, more or less directly, to the efforts of a collectivity to safeguard its moral and material interests. It applies, for example, to a tax of general utility like the *commun de la paix*, or to a contribution voted by the entire population of a town, or to resources enjoyed by all the inhabitants of a given place (grazing rights, etc.), or to a group formed to defend its security and its rights, or to safeguard religion and the Church. It became part of ecclesiastical vocabulary very early on, and can designate church property or a community of clergy.

In fact, the word 'commune' evokes the idea not so much of an independent government as of a group formed to watch over collective interests. We reach the same conclusion if we examine the etymology and origins of the word *commune*, together with the meanings they suggest.

A theory has been advanced that the formation of the word *communia*, from which the Romance word *commune* derives, occurred as a result of substituting a feminine singular noun for a plural adjective signifying the customary rights of the community, [*jura*] *communia*. It is also claimed that *regalia*, a feminine noun (though a rare one), *régale* in French, comes from [*jura*] *regalia*. According to this theory the commune means the combined rights of the community.

This hypothesis strikes me as unacceptable. In the twelfth and thirteenth centuries, a classical Latin word, *communio*, which means an association or mutual participation and cannot be explained by the expression *jura communia*, is used alongside the Low Latin noun *communia*, with which it is interchangeable. *Communio*, which is purer Latin, is preferred by some of the drafters of charters, and by certain authors, for example Guibert de Nogent.

There also occurs, in classical Latin texts, a word which cannot be the direct ancestor of the French *commune* despite their identical spelling, but from which the Romance word *commun* is derived, namely the neuter substantive *commune*. It appears in the sense of 'people with common interests' in Cicero (*commune Milyadum, commune Siciliae, commune Cretensium*), in Ovid (*commune Pelasgae gentis*), and on coins (*commune Asiae*). In an inscription dated 169 AD it means an association (*commune mimorum*). The word *communia* may have been fashioned from the Romance word *commun* which derives from this, just as *parlamentum* was made from *parlement*. Du Cange, after citing the Low Latin *commune* with the meaning of "contribution towards the keeping of the peace", classifies under the same head the Latin words *commune, communia* and *communitas*, all of which can designate a human community.

In any case, in twelfth-century colloquial speech the Romance word *commune*, derived from the Low Latin *communia*, meant, like the classical Latin *commune*, a people with interests in common, or an association, as is evident when Wace[1] writes:

Assez tost oï Ricars dire
Ke vilain commuigne faisoient
Et ses droitures li tauroient.
[Soon Richard heard tell that the
villeins were banding together to deprive him
of his prerogatives.]

The *commuigne* means here the inhabitants as a body rising up against the lord. In another passage of Wace, *commune* means peace, unity:

N'en out entr'els pais ne commune.
[There was neither peace nor harmony between them.]

The foregoing discussion provides a reasonably good starting point. But these are only preliminary enquiries. The surest way of discovering what it was that distinguished a town called a commune from other towns is to find out both what was meant and what was intended by the lords and kings when they declared they were 'ratifying', 'granting', or 'allowing' the commune to the burgesses of a given town. We may then learn what a commune is, or at least what it is not, and a solution will be in sight.

Communes were first granted in France at the end of the eleventh century. We need not go further back than this. Work on the English borough requires research into more ancient documents; although the

---

[1]Wace of Jersey (c. 1100–1175) wrote long historical poems in Anglo-Norman. Of particular interest is his *Roman de brut*, dedicated to Eleanor of Aquitaine. (Translator's note.)

disastrous decline of urban life in the Roman provinces as a result of the invasions affected Britain as well as Gaul, the English borough existed in Anglo-Saxon times. But in France during the early Middle Ages there is no sign of the commune, for the very good reason that the town may be said to have almost lost its historic role. The difference arose from political causes; the economic causes – commercial collapse, formation of a strong, closed domanial economy – operated on both sides of the Channel. Whereas the Anglo-Saxon kings wielded considerable influence over the destiny of urban groups and kept alive a certain number of fortified towns, which were surrounded by an ancient Roman enceinte, by using them as fortresses and administrative centres, rulers in northern Gaul stopped using the towns for political purposes. The short-lived Carolingian renaissance failed to preserve them. Those which had not completely disappeared lost the attraction they had possessed under the Merovingians; their monuments fell into ruin; the roads were neglected; many of them were partly destroyed by Norse raiders; in fact their only use in the ninth century was as a shelter for peasants who happened to be working nearby, or as a rather dubious refuge when danger threatened.

The only towns with any vestige of life were the episcopal cities: so far as one can ascertain from the scanty evidence available, these remained centres of ecclesiastical administration and of domanial cultivation. The modest groups of dwellings which grew up near some of the monasteries or fortified castles, and were the homes of scholars, monks or warriors, with their attendant serfs who provided them with clothes or arms, had no pretensions whatever to municipal status. It would seem (though this is open to question) that in northern Gaul there was no bourgeoisie engaged in trade; there were no special laws to protect the inhabitants of borough or walled town.

In the tenth century, certainly from the eleventh century onwards, the picture gradually changes. The closed domanial economy without markets is no longer the normal pattern of material existence. Urban industries spring up. Traders are no longer nomadic, like those seedy traffickers against whom the Angle-Saxon kings had taken precautions. Markets were created, to which farmers brought produce and drove cattle. Different kinds of produce changed hands, so that the people's diet became more varied and they ceased to live from hand to mouth. In fact, it was the beginning of urban life. Moreover, as F. Lot observed, the growth of communal liberties did not depend solely on economic revival and could occur in towns without a suburb peopled with artisans. It was the desire to resist their bishop which led the inhabitants of Cambrai to form a sworn association, a *conjuratio*, which was certainly an early example of a communal undertaking. This event occurred in 958. A century later the history of the French communes began.

As regards the geographical limits of this study, I shall only rarely use examples from countries where Provençal was spoken. Towns in this area are seldom called communes. Ernest Roschach and Auguste Molinier included studies of *La commune de Toulouse* in the new edition of the *Histoire du Languedoc*, and M. R. Limouzin-Lamothe gave his thesis the same title. But the sources they use mention only an *urbs*, a *suburbium*, a *civitas*, a *universitas*, but no *communia*. Moreover, when they cited the charter of 1152 setting up a *commune consilium Tolose civitatis et suburbii*, they failed to notice that it forbade the inhabitants, on pain of being brought before the count's court of justice, to "conspire together to lend each other mutual assistance", which was precisely the essence of the communal bond. It must be admitted that *Les Etablissements de Rouen* had penetrated as far as southern Aquitaine, to Bayonne, and that Bordeaux became a commune when it was besieged by the king of Castile in 1206. But, generally speaking, the political development of the southern towns in the twelfth century was unconnected with the growth of towns which had received their liberties in the centre and north of the kingdom, from Poitou to Picardy. It is mainly in these towns that we must study the historical phenomenon of the commune. Brittany may be ignored for this purpose, for it had no communes in the Middle Ages, apart from an abortive attempt by the inhabitants of Saint-Malo in the early fourteenth century.

The Flemish towns, except for Saint-Omer, Aire and Courtrai, are not referred to as communes in contemporary documents, and it is best to exclude from this study – to avoid confusion and obscurity – towns which had such an unusual municipal development. Strictly speaking, they never received a charter granting them a commune, although at the outset they were no different from the French communes. They were at first sworn associations, and their *keure*, their *loi* was a charter embodying practices similar to those of the communes: justice was administered both by the *koremanni* (*jurés*) and by the seigneurial tribunal of echevins. But the attempted reaction towards centralization which marked the reign of the count of Flanders, Philip of Alsace (1168–1181), put an end to the parallel development of communes and *villes à loi*. For Philip's action resulted in the discomfiture of the counts, and the great Flemish towns of the thirteenth and fourteenth centuries became something akin to republics. I do not propose to include them in this enquiry.

Despite these restrictions imposed by chronological and geographical factors, we can still, for the purposes of this study, draw on a sufficiently large collection of seigneurial and royal charters: those of paramount importance being the charters of Philip Augustus, those of the English princes of the Angevin dynasty and, standing out from the rather scanty group of the other seigneurial charters, the collection of acts of the counts of Ponthieu.

It is tempting to be more precise and to close this preamble with a list of the French communes in the Middle Ages. Such an attempt would be both difficult and premature. Du Cange and his continuator Dom Carpentier, under 'Communes', suggested a catalogue of 135 communes, which could be reduced to 129 by excluding six names from the Dauphiné and Bresse which became French rather late. But, as Bréquigny had already observed, they included in their list names of towns which were not communes, and on the other hand they omitted many authentic communes. Even so, this early, well-documented study, could well serve as a starting point for further work. Yet, except for J. Brissaud, who tried to draw up a list of charters granting communes, not one of the scholars who have concerned themselves with the history of the communes has taken up the idea of the catalogue attempted by Du Cange and Carpentier; and one's first impression on reading the various studies on the subject of communes is one of slight surprise that their authors do not even try to give an approximate figure. Were there 150 communes, or 500?

One reason why historians have avoided hazarding a hypothesis is probably the impossibility of determining a figure for the whole of the Middle Ages. In fact the communes evolved over three centuries. Some were already in existence in the eleventh century, but others were founded or reconstituted when the movement itself was in decline, in the mid-fourteenth century or even in the fifteenth century. On the other hand, many of them had a very brief life, for reasons not always known to us, or else they found, in the long run, that the Paris Parlement denied them the right to exist. And, lastly, there are others which expired and then revived. Nothing is more changeable than the list of the French communes. However, it must be remembered that the relevant archives are still being worked on, and they probably have some surprises in store. We must await the completion of the series of volumes of communal charters and customs which is being published by the Société d'Histoire du Droit, and also of the *Recueil des documents rélatifs à l'histoire du droit municipal en France*. Only then will a future generation of historians be able to draw up the list of communes. But they will have to conform to the ideas and keep to the vocabulary of the burgesses and jurists of the Middle Ages, so that they apply the word 'commune' only to what they did. We shall now examine what, in fact, they did mean by this term.

3. The grant: constitutive element of a commune

"We have granted a commune to the inhabitants of such-and-such a town." These are usually the opening words of the charter granted by the king or the lord in the late eleventh century and in the twelfth century. Nothing in the body of the text shows that the commune consists of any specific institutions, particularly administrative ones; the link between these two elements was not established until later theories arrived at by jurists. These documents do, it is true, state that they grant or allow a commune "with the customs" or "with the customs and other points contained in what follows". After this comes a list of the articles of civil and penal law, very rarely a statement of constitutional arrangements, and very frequently an enumeration of the time-honoured customs or the rules which could be used to put an end to protracted litigation and prevent fresh strife between burgesses of the communal group and their lord or his officers. But expressions such as *cum consuetudinibus*, or *ad consuetudines et puncta* are not explanations of or enlargements upon the word *communia*, and whenever *ad* is used instead of *cum*, it still means 'with'.

The proof of this assertion is what follows. First, many of these texts make it certain that municipal life was already functioning before the commune was instituted. We know that the Carolingian *échevinage* existed in many localities in northern France and was capable of change and adaptation; indeed we have indications that the twelfth-century associations – gilds, brotherhoods, charities – could provide leaders and models of collective institutions in the towns where they functioned. Roger Grand has given us a most able description of those pre-communal times (which can only be brought to life by a great effort of the imagination), when an elite composed of experienced men was formed to meet the common needs: they built bridges, markets, fortifications, and churches; they fixed the tariffs, they administered the *métiers* (trades or crafts). The inertia of the lord, particularly if he was a layman, was a distinct advantage to them and permitted the emergence of the earliest

urban liberties outside his control. It is hardly surprising that the privilege
of a commune was superimposed on franchises already in existence,
which the burgesses merely wished to have confirmed. It so happens that
we have unambiguous proof of this. In 1188 the burgesses of Tournai
received from Philip Augustus "the institution of peace and of a
commune, with the same usages and customs which the aforesaid
burgesses had possessed *before the institution of the commune*". Then
follows the enumeration of these former customs: the frequent
occurrence of the words *commune* or *hommes de la commune* in this
enumeration results from an unfortunate choice of terms whereby the
situation preceding the granting of the charter by Philip Augustus was
confused with the situation it created.

In cases like this it sometimes happens that the former customs thus
ratified are not listed. For example, in the very brief charter granted to the
burgesses of Montreuil-sur-Mer in 1188, Philip Augustus gives them "the
commune, with the practices and customs they are known to have had
before", but he does not enumerate them. The following year the same
omission may be observed in the charter he granted to the burgesses of
Saint-Riquier, which had been constituted a commune by Louis VI: he
allows them to maintain the "reasonable customs" they had before; he
merely adds that they will be able to "create a mayor in their commune as
often as they wish and judge expedient".

In the early days of the communal movement, about 1108, when
Baudry, bishop of Noyon, set up a commune in his city and had it ratified
by pope and king, he informed all Christians of this fact in a very brief
charter containing not a word about the administration of the town nor
about the public or private laws which the burgesses would be expected to
follow. Louis VII was no more explicit when, in 1140, he had the
commune sworn in and undertook to respect it; but it is quite possible that
jurés of Noyon were not instituted until the middle of the century.

At the beginning of the twelfth century, Guillaume Talevas, count of
Ponthieu, sold the burgesses of Abbeville the right to form a commune,
but gave them no *scriptum authenticum*; it was not until 1184 that they had
a charter granting them rights and customs, on the model of Amiens,
Corbie and Saint-Quentin. In the case of the town of Saint-Omer, the
permission granted in 1127 by William Clito, count of Flanders, to
preserve the commune, is completely distinct from the granting of certain
juridical, judiciary or commercial customs. The count said: "I grant the
aforementioned laws and customs", and later: "I ordain that their
commune continue to exist as it was sworn, and I do not permit it to be

dissolved by anyone". In 1181 Philip Augustus declared that he ratified the commune granted to the burgesses of Soissons by his grandfather Louis VI, and that he ratified their customs in the form granted them by his father Louis VII. Gautier Tirel, when granting a charter to the burgesses of Poix in 1208, resorted to this characteristic formula, after declaring he granted the commune: "And now we must enumerate the constitutions of the commune article by article." In 1227 Thibaud IV, count of Champagne, granted a commune to the inhabitants of Fismes in these words: "First, the men have sworn enduring allegiance to me, and have also sworn to come to each other's help so far as is in their power. And here follow, on the other hand (*sunt autem*), the institutions of this commune . . . . ." In the case of Poitiers the distinction between granting a commune and granting liberties is even more clearly drawn: in 1199 Queen Eleanor granted or ratified liberties to the inhabitants, and granted them a commune in a second charter. Philip Augustus drew the same distinction in his confirmatory charter of 1204.

And so it is clear that the privilege of a commune existed in its own right, apart from any granting of liberties; it could be granted in isolation, and it could even be granted without a charter.

Finally, as will emerge from a subsequent chapter, the institutions of some communes might well be less liberal than those of towns enjoying wide liberties, but which had not been authorized to form a sworn association of burgesses; in fact, we shall see that it was even possible, as in the case of Rheims, for identical institutions to persist over a number of years, whether or not the town enjoyed the privilege of a commune. The idea of a commune was not inevitably bound up with the idea of administrative independence. We must therefore cease to consider the commune in the light of municipal liberties. It may have coincided with political, judiciary and financial autonomy, and it may even have helped to obtain this; but independence is not its essence. It therefore becomes imperative to discover precisely what was granted with the granting of a commune.

The only explanation which smooths out the difficulties and contradictions in the texts is that the granting of a commune was a much more simple matter than historians suppose, and that *the only factor involved was the communal bond.* Two sets of documents, one concerning the little commune of Chelles, near Paris, and the other the attempts of the burgesses of Châteauneuf-de-Tours to set up a commune, confirm this hypothesis with a finality which has not hitherto struck historians forcibly enough.

Chelles, *Cala juxta Parisius*, figures in the official list of *communie* drawn up by Philip Augustus, and a charter of 1189–1190 has been preserved, inserted in registers E and F of the *Trésor des Chartes*, in which Philip Augustus records a transaction between the commune and the abbess of Chelles, *inter abbatissam Cale et communiam ejusdem ville.* In 1271, the Paris Parlement acknowledged afresh the existence of the commune of Chelles and decided in its favour in a lawsuit it was engaged in against the convent. The abbess, in an agreement reached that year, did not deny that the inhabitants were *gens de commune.* They showed her letters to the guard of the prévôté of Paris when, in 1303, he was instructed to inquire into their rights, and they declared, on the basis of this document and "the king's registers", that they possessed "a corporate body and commune, and a seal proper to a commune which they and their predecessors had used for a hundred and eighty years". Obviously their rights had begun to be contested. Fifteen years before, the abbess succeeded in obtaining a decree from the Parlement whereby "the people of Chelles lost their status of mayor and commune, because they had no privilege", meaning a charter expressly granting them a commune. But if that charter did not exist, what was the concession which had led them to believe they had constituted a commune "for a hundred and eighty years"? The only one known to me is the charter granted them by Louis the Fat in 1128. In it he declared, "We desire, we approve and ratify by royal authority the oaths and confederations whereby the men of Chelles have federated and bound themselves to each other, *inter se invicem confederati sunt et ligati*, saving their fealty to us and all the just customs of the church of Sainte-Bathilde". And he grants them, without specifying what they are, all the good customs they had in the time of King Philip I, adding that they could if need be have them attested by four aged, loyal residents of Chelles. He adds that no one must ever be arrested at Chelles without a reason and without trial. He makes no mention of the word commune. But it was assumed from that date that Chelles had a commune. If this means anything, it must mean that the one element which was enough to constitute a commune was the oath binding the inhabitants and acknowledged by the lord.

The inhabitants of Châteauneuf, a small town near Tours not to be confused with Châteauneuf-sur-Loire, were at the same time subjects of the chapter of St Martin's, of the king of France in his capacity of abbot of St Martin's, and of the count of Anjou. For two centuries they strove unsuccessfully to form a commune. As early as 1122 there was a "war between the rebellious burgesses and the canons". On his return from

Toulouse in 1141, Louis VII stopped at Tours and settled their differences for a time by means of concessions which the men of Châteauneuf paid for in cash. Emboldened by his kindness, they forged a royal charter, or at least made alterations in a charter already in their possession, which has not been preserved. This document stated that Louis VII had ratified the customs of their *universitas*, settled in their favour certain legal disputes, and engaged them to remain confederated and bound to one another: *confederati sitis et inter vos ligati*. We learn from a letter written in 1180 by John of Salisbury, then bishop of Chartres, that the inhabitants of Châteauneuf were at this time bound by an oath, but it had been sworn in secret, with the aim of uniting them against the chapter of St Martin's of Tours. John of Salisbury was instructed to give them a canonical reprimand, and they were obliged to renounce their oath. It was at this time that the so-called charter of Louis VII urging them to remain confederated and bound to each other was declared to be false. In 1181 the young Philip Augustus, instead of bearing them a grudge for this forgery – which was after all a venial sin in the Middle Ages – granted "to all the burgesses of St Martin living in Châteauneuf" a charter which has, incidentally, been described inaccurately as granting a commune. In fact, the king merely confirmed a collective guarantee which had been granted them by Louis VII against any fiscal exactions, and he also permitted their finances to be administered by ten men of integrity (*prud'hommes*).

Even though the collective guarantee granted by Louis VII is called *communitas* in Philip Augustus' document, and although it is sometimes permissible as early as the twelfth century to regard *communa* and *communitas* as interchangeable terms, the way the text is composed makes it perfectly clear that the granting of a *communitas* by Louis VII was not a granting of a commune but merely a fiscal privilege common to all burgesses. In the second part of the charter, which is absent from Louis VII's document, Philip Augustus declares that oaths must be sworn. But these oaths are, on the one hand an oath of obedience to the *prud'hommes* in all their decisions regarding expenditure, on the other hand an oath whereby the *prud'hommes* undertake to administer justly; the question of an oath of communal confederation does not arise. The burgesses did not invoke this charter of 1181 to claim that the king had allowed them to form a commune, but they chose to ignore the fact that John of Salisbury had obliged them to go back on their oath.

In the event, in 1184, William of the White Hands, with Henry, abbot of Marmoutier, were commissioned by the pope to go to Châteauneuf to repossess the canons of St Martin's of Tours in their rights, and to oblige the burgesses of Châteauneuf to give up the "commune or conjuration which the said burgesses were said to have set up". William brought both sides together, but without success. But one day, as he was sitting in the chapter-house at St Martin's "a great crowd of common people" came in to complain of the prominent burgesses of the town who had set up the commune. The archbishop, who thought this incident little short of miraculous, went out into the cloister garth, and there "a countless multitude" assembled and complained "that certain burgesses of Châteauneuf had improperly burdened them with *tailles* and other exactions. They maintained that the aforesaid burgesses had used threats and violence to force them to swear certain oaths so as to gain control over them. They requested insistently to be released from the illegal oaths they had sworn". Archbishop William then read out to the crowd the document whereby the pope, mindful of the privileges of St Martin's of Tours, quashed "any oath which the burgesses of Châteauneuf have sworn under the name of commune and by common oath, by whatever name it is known". The pope excommunicated any of those involved who refused to abjure the oath, and quashed "the oath whereby the people had rashly bound themselves to them", commanding penances to be imposed on those who had sworn the oath, which was said to be destructive of the liberties of the Church as regards the exercise of justice.

Then the archbishop read out letters from King Philip Augustus to the burgesses of Châteauneuf. In them the king reported that Pope Lucius III informed him that he had "quashed a commune and a common conjuration", *communiam et quamdam communem conjurationem*, made by the burgesses of Châteauneuf to the detriment of St Martin's of Tours. Philip Augustus enjoined them to give up this commune: *ut ab hujusmodi communia cessetis*; he did not deprive them of the liberties he had granted them in 1181.

After reading out these letters, the prelate released the populace from their oath, forbade them to respond to demands for *tailles*, for contributions to expenses of the watch or any other exactions, and forbade them to comply with any legal citations made by the instigators of the conjuration. The common people then abjured the oath they had sworn. Finally, the archbishop summoned to appear before him the powerful burgesses, *potentiores burgenses*, the authors and instigators of the conjuration and the common oath: Thomas d'Amboise, Philippe Annier, Nicolas Engelard, Péan Gatineau "and many others". They had to swear not to observe the commune and the conjuration they had made in the form of an oath in common. The archbishop forbade these notables to levy any more *tailles* or exactions in future or to usurp the judicial functions of St Martin's of Tours.

The meticulous chronicler of Tours confirms these facts and supplies the date: "On 24 February 1185", he says, "the burgesses of Châteauneuf renounced the commune they had sworn against the church of St Martin of Tours."

On 17 April a papal bull ratified "the renunciation of the commune or conjuration", *abjuratio communie vel conjurationis*. But not until the conquest of Anjou in 1212 did a royal charter suppress the rule of the ten elected just men (*prud'hommes*) which was instituted in 1181; the oath sworn by the inhabitants to the ten elected men became void *ipso facto*, but still, the fact was specifically stated: any kind of oath which was in any way binding on the burgesses of Châteauneuf seemed dangerous. "The ten sworn men (*jurés*) for the community of the town and the oaths sworn by the others to these ten *jurés* are abolished, and henceforward there will be neither commune, nor common oath, nor common obligation." In 1305, at a time when, as we shall see, the status of communes had just been determined by jurists and rested on the idea of a legal personality and the possession of a charter, the inhabitants of Châteauneuf rebelled yet again. We learn from letters written by Philip the Fair that they banded together "under cover of the confraternity of St Eloi", hatched a conspiracy by binding themselves on oath, and "usurped the name of commune . . . although they had no right or privilege to form *corps et collège*". The uprising was put down, a ruinous fine imposed on the rebels, and the confraternity disbanded. That was their last attempt.

The inherent interest of this history of the abortive Châteauneuf commune needs no stressing. At a period when communal revolution had become a thing of the past, a small bourgeois oligarchy insisted on forming a commune as a sure means of resisting an ecclesiastical lordship and of imposing its selfish wishes on the inhabitants as a whole. At a very late date, in the reign of Philip the Fair, a fresh attempt was made. But at no point do the texts imply that a specific administrative organization accompanied the formation of the Châteauneuf commune. It is a perfect example of the commune stripped of inessentials. It was a sworn association, and nothing else.

If, in the light of these texts concerning Chelles and Châteauneuf, we look again at the charters in which French kings and feudal lords granted a commune, right down to St Louis' day, we shall find that all the documents agree on one point. The act of granting a commune to the burgesses of a town implied the permission – for reasons we shall examine later – to form an association, to bind themselves together on oath. It might also be an opportunity to ratify their customs or to grant them new liberties; but these things were merely extras, not an essential part of the contract. The only definition of the granting of a commune in the twelfth century is the permission to form a sworn association. Without a sworn association there was no commune, and this association was a sufficient basis for a commune. The word 'commune' means exactly the same as 'common oath'.

I advance no claim to have discovered the historical importance of the communal oath (which would rank alongside the discovery of America!); however, the existence of conflicting definitions of the commune and the failure to recognize any difference between a commune and a town with extensive franchises, encourage me to hope that the foregoing discussion has proved useful. Furthermore, if the granting of a commune is correctly understood, several difficulties are resolved. It becomes clear why many communes enjoy no more liberties, or even less, than *villes de franchises*; it becomes clear why the charter granting the commune so rarely sets out the workings of municipal institutions; and it is clear why there are communes without a charter at all.

CHAPTER 2

Commune charters and franchise charters.
The part played by the commune in urban
emancipation

1. Available documents

At this point the following objection will be raised: you have shown that
the essential element, the indispensable element which is sufficient for the
granting of a commune, was the permission to form an association;
indeed, this explains why there is often no other accompanying element,
and why the concession may be restricted to giving this permission,
sometimes even without stating it in writing. But in many cases, even in
the early days of the communal institution, it was accompanied by certain
liberties, and the commune was a more complex affair than you maintain;
the Middle Ages were full of variety, and it is hardly surprising if the act of
granting a commune was sometimes straightforward and at other times
more complicated, as when it was agreed to make the commune a
powerful and independent political entity. In short (it will be asked) what
is the objection to accpeting, on two points at least, the theory advanced
in Bréquigny's *Recherches sur les communes*, concerning the "distinctive
characteristics of what we call commune"? He states that "the first is the
sworn association" and that another is "the attribution of rights and
privileges, which always included a more or less extensive jurisdiction
placed in the hands of magistrates of the commune whom it chooses
itself".

Such an objection may well be based on the formula "with the customs
which follow", etc., which is often found at the beginning of the charter.
This objection will be met by showing that the clauses mentioning
liberties supposedly specific to the commune are neither essential nor

always special, and that on the other hand some of the liberties not enjoyed by *villes franches* are not present either in certain communes.

At this point in our enquiry it therefore seems indispensable to compare the commune charters with the charters granting franchises. But the reader must not be faced with an assortment of documents of very different dates. It has been possible, so far, to conduct the argument on the basis of texts spanning several centuries of history, but we must now turn our attention to the earliest period, the end of the eleventh century and the twelfth century. Only by adopting this method shall we arrive at the facts. It is not possible to compare commune charters of one period with franchise charters of some other period. What must engage our attention is the earliest period when the movement towards liberation can be glimpsed in its original spontaneity and purity, before it was distorted by the classifications of contemporary jurists, or corrupted by the advance of monarchical policies.

Not many of these early communal charters have come down to us. Those granted by Louis VI (the Fat) are the most valuable: we have the charters of Laon, Noyon, Soissons, and Corbie, either in the original or in Philip Augustus' ratifications, which leave no doubt of the accuracy of the reproduction, and we even possess the original of the rural federation of Bruyères-en-Laonnois, modelled on that of Laon. The charters granted by Louis VII to the burgesses of Mantes and Beauvais, and the one granted by Philip Augustus to the rural federation of Vailly-en-Soissonnais, also reproduce those of Louis the Fat. Louis VII's charters for Compiègne and Senlis have been preserved in the original. Philip Augustus, in the early years of his reign (1188), acknowledged, by a special concession, the commune already in existence at Tournai. Also, from the north of France we have the charters granted by the counts of Flanders to Saint-Omer, Aire, and Arras, by the count of Ponthieu to Abbeville, and by the count of Eu to the town of Eu. The count of Champagne gave a commune to the town of Meaux, the count of Beaumont-sur-Oise gave one to the fortress of Chambly, the count of Dreux recognised the commune which the burgesses of the town had already formed in Louis VI's time. Some of these seigneurial charters have come down to us in the original, others contain a reproduction of customs of an earlier date. The original form of the charters of Amiens and Péronne is not known, and they will be used in this inquiry only as corroborative evidence.

If we add to these commune charters the interesting account of the former customs of the town of Ham, and the 'rescript' drawn up between

1160 and 1170, which represents the earliest version of the *Établissements de Rouen*, we have at our disposal a score of twelfth-century documents which provide ample evidence on the earliest communal liberties. The list of franchise charters in the twelfth century is much longer, which makes it impossible to mention each one individually. The only comparisons we need to make are between documents of similar type. As early as the first half of the twelfth century a certain number of towns in the royal domain and in the duchy of Normandy acquired liberties in some ways comparable to those enjoyed by the communes, and this is the important fact. The king-dukes, Henry I Beauclerc and Henry II Plantagenet, granted to the town of Verneuil, before it became a commune, two important sets of customs. The charters of La Chapelle-la-Reine, Bourges, Étampes, Orléans, Sceaux-en-Gatinais and Lorris date from the reign of Louis VI. In Louis VII's reign and early in the reign of Philip Augustus were granted the royal or seigneurial charters of Saint-Germain-des-Bois, les Alluets, Tonnerre, La Bruyère, Bonvilliers, Châteauneuf-sur-Loire, Méru, Auxerre, Charost, Blois, Villeneuve-Saint-Melon, etc., and lastly Beaumont-en-Argonne and Rheims. These are the charters we shall examine.

2. Comparison between commune charters and franchise charters

The question whether the franchise charters were, on the whole, a later phenomenon than commune charters, is a difficult one to answer, even if we assume we possess all the documents worth comparing with each other. Luchaire cites as the oldest franchise charters those of Morville-sur-Seille (967), La Chapelle-Aude (1073), Orleans (1057) and Angers (1135). But the inhabitants of Morville (who were in any case the subjects of the emperor and not the king of France) merely acquired freedom from serfdom; the customs of La Chapelle-Aude were established mainly to determine the rights to be enjoyed by the monks; the earliest Orleans charter was granted by Henry I to protect the inhabitants during the grape harvest, and the Angers charter was granted by the count in favour of the Angers vine-growers. The charter granted by Matthew I, count of Beaumont-sur-Oise falls in the same category, in that it offered protection to the inhabitants of Bernes against the exactions of the provost (1110). The charter granted by Émenon and Foulque, princes of Issoudun, in 984, to the abbey of Notre-Dame, did not bestow freedoms on the town, which did not in fact acquire a charter until much later: this one merely removed certain burdens such as military service, from the inhabitants of the small town of Saint-Martin which lay outside the ramparts of Issoudun. These various documents are not interesting enough to be taken into account. On the other hand, the charter of the commune of Laon was not perhaps the first of its kind, and we have seen that communes were formed much earlier, at Cambrai in 1076, at Le Mans as early as 1039. But, all things considered, it is impossible to regard the communal movement as anterior to the granting of genuine charters of franchise. The two things overlapped rather than followed each other. The formation of sworn associations certainly had enormous influence; it gave the nobles food for thought and prompted some of them to make concessions. But it did no more than foster an inevitable and necessary change. In any case, chronology lends no support to the theory that the charters of franchise are a more or less pale imitation of the commune charters.

We must see whether a clear distinction can be drawn between these two types of charter, by making a textual comparison between the two as to length and internal organisation. It is possible to state, on the evidence of such original texts as have come down to us, that the chanceries regarded both kinds of document as of equal importance and solemnity. The franchise charters, at least those which emerged from the royal chancery, were drawn up, like the commune charters, in the solemn form of a diploma and began with an invocation. There was no general rule governing the length of the charter, a feature which indicates more than anything the energy and ambition of the inhabitants, the goodwill of the lord and the ability of his subjects to pay more or less dearly for his favours. As early as the twelfth century there were franchise charters of considerable length, for example the Lorris charter, which owes its existence to the particular goodwill of Louis VI and Louis VII, and also the famous charter of Beaumont-en-Argonne, which is even more liberal and comprehensive; by contrast, the members of the Corbie commune were satisfied with a few guarantees of justice and security and the members of the Eu commune made do with just two clauses. Generally speaking the passage of time accentuated the tendency of the recipients to be easily satisfied or more demanding, as the case might be. However, there is no reliable pattern enabling us to distinguish between commune charters and franchise charters.

It is not their method of setting out the facts either; if, indeed, one may use such an expression in reference to documents which exhibit disorder rather than method and incoherence rather than a sense of proportion and discrimination. Both the commune charters and the franchise charters read like improvisations. Their writers were not open to political ideas capable of forming a basis for rational claims, and so the documents are full of obscurities, contradictions and puerilities. They conjure up sittings of the commune commission at which the speakers had an eye mainly to their immediate interests of the moment, no matter how petty, and insisted on the inclusion of clauses which occurred to them on the spur of the moment or were inspired by what one of them had read in other local charters he had managed to see. Very often those present wished to settle a question currently under litigation, or were prompted by the memory of some unfortunate incident. At Roye, a pastrycook had poisoned his customers: by the terms of the commune charter, the mayor is entitled to forbid the making of harmful cakes. At Orléans, carts caused traffic jams when they went through the Dunois gate to bring in food supplies, and so the franchise charter of 1178 contained an article ordering carts to make room for others as soon as they had been unloaded. On the other hand, it is rarely stated by what administrative rules the town is to be governed. Whether one considers the commune charters or the franchise charters, the modest nature of their demands is a feature common to both.

There is no essential difference between the social categories to which these two types of charter are addressed. We must not be dominated by the conventional idea of the Flemish free towns (*villes libres*) where industry and commerce were remarkably flourishing. We must not imagine that the communes were necessarily in this state or that the main body of the population was markedly different from the population of the *villes de franchise*. First, as I have shown, there were communes which were little rural boroughs or federations of villages. In addition, even in towns of some size like Soissons, Senlis, Saint-Quentin, Dijon, rural tradition had persisted; a considerable number of the burgesses still followed a semi-agricultural way of life, just as they had in the *villes de franchise* like Lorris or Beaumont-en-Argonne. Nor should this surprise us. In the twelfth century, from the Somme to the Loire, which was the area where almost all the earliest communes came into being, the development of urban life was a recent phenomenon. In the tenth century the only way of life known in this area was agricultural. The towns owed their revival not only to the resumption of trade and export industry; it was often a result of the safety now afforded to agricultural workers by the ramparts and defences. Exhausted by constant brigandage, many of them made sure that their homes were in a fortified place, while they tended their fields and vineyards close by. Others settled in the town itself and opened stalls where they sometimes made their fortune, but they never gave up their land. It is clear from the texts that many of the towns which obtained either commune charters or franchise charters were, in fact, large villages in which rustic dwellings with farmyards, cowsheds and vegetable patches, existed alongside solid stone houses. Even in industrial towns like Sens, Saint-Quentin or Péronne, economic prosperity was for the most part based on agriculture. Careful examination of the charters of Saint-Quentin, Roye, Bray-sur-Somme and the customs of Ham reveals a clause granting long holidays to those burgesses who wished to tend their land; they were obliged to reside in the town so as to retain their privileges as burgesses, but they had permission to take long leaves of absence "for their March" and "for their August"; in fact they could spend more than half the year on the land.

In short, the people who obtained communal charters were not necessarily traders and artisans absorbed by their jobs. Their distinguishing feature was that they possessed great energy, and had had recourse to the revolutionary method of conjuration to attain their object; or else they had been fortunate enough to be favoured by a lenient overlord. It is natural that they should share the same tastes and feel the same needs as the recipients of franchise charters, that they should have asked for the same things, and that there should be no marked difference between the two types of institution or their charters.

Let us turn our attention to the contents of the two kinds of charter. The clause concerning the oath of mutual help does not, of course, occur in the charters of the towns without a commune, but the burgess of the free town is also a privileged person, a member of a community with a set procedure for joining or leaving it. The communal charter of Laon lays on the burgesses the obligation to own a house, or a vine, or enough chattels to enable them, if need be, to satisfy the law. But the same is true of Verneuil before the town had become a commune: the duke of Normandy guaranteed that each burgess should have three acres of ground and a garden and he must own a house and pay a due on it, *ut inde fiat burgensis*. In the towns governed by the law of Beaumont, the new burgess receives a hut and a piece of land. As Bréquigny saw quite clearly, both in the town of burgesses only and in the town with a commune, "the burgess' rights were substantially the same". He adds: "The only difference related to the extent of the privileges." But the extent of the privileges, as will be seen, is very far from differentiating between a type of very favoured towns, namely the communes, and a class of less favoured towns, the *villes franches*. The truth is far more complex. The primary benefit conferred by entering either free town or commune is security. The suzerain granting the charter refrains from acts of violence and extortions, and guarantees to each man his possessions. The most numerous and most detailed clauses in both types of charter are of a legal nature. There are to be no improper writs of summons, no arbitrary arrests, no ill-usage in the rare event of being imprisoned while awaiting trial (bail was in common use). Rules of procedure are to be respected; in particular, a man may not be tried outside his own town. People were reluctant to be summoned outside the town by the overlord, or to risk wasting time finding judges who did not know them. Even at Orléans, where the burgesses' liberties were so strictly curtailed for a long period, the 1138 charter forbids, during the entire course of the trial, forcible detention of the burgess summoned before the king's court, and the 1183 charter grants the natives of Orléans the right not to be summoned any further afield than Étampes, Lorris or Yèvres. In many charters of the free towns and communes, punishments are regulated, the scale of the fines is fixed and controlled; legal duelling is seldom suppressed, but its abuses are attenuated. The so-called *paix du marché*, 'market peace', is firmly established: anyone going to the fair or to market must not be arrested or otherwise molested.

Perusal of these charters granting communes or franchises, therefore, gives the impression that behind the burgesses' demands lay the desire not to be ill-treated by the royal officers, not to be arrested or punished unjustly, and not to be roughly handled for mere trifles. There was also the wish not to be burdened with arbitrary taxes, levies and forced labour (*corvées*). The demands made by the lord, the market tax, coinage rights, bans and *banalités*, levies, watch duty and military service, are the subject of very varied clauses, which regulate some taxes and abolish others. No absolute distinction can be drawn between the two types of charter. The *villes de franchise*, like the communes, obtain major fiscal concessions. For example, the *taille* is abolished in the customs of Lorris, the charters of Bourges, Orléans, Tonnerre, Auxerre, etc., and in those of Saint-Omer and Mantes. It is true that the guarantees provided against the king's officers or the lord were not always effective, and the *villes de franchise* still had a *prévôt* who might be, even as late as St Louis' reign, an unbearable tyrant with scant inclination to respect the charter; but the communes, as we shall see, had not all got rid of their *prévôt*, and there were some which did not enjoy financial autonomy.

Nor was it possible, in the twelfth century, to draw a radical distinction between commune and free town on the grounds of military obligations towards king or lord. During almost the whole of the first century of their history, their obligations in this respect were similar, namely an agreed undertaking that all subjects, even the commonalty, must help their lord and no one else (it was particularly necessary to stress this point because in the eleventh century some lords did not scruple to levy by force men living outside their territory). Exceptions and attenuations are encountered in both types of charter. Before the reign of Philip Augustus, the obligation to military service varied widely between one town and another. But he hit on the idea of the militarized commune; it was he who adopted the formula of the redemption of military service in the case of the free towns and the unredeemable service in the case of the communal militia. There is no doubt that, in the minds of the men granted the earliest commune charters, there was no intention of attributing to the *communia* a specific military role. Matthew III, count of Beaumont-sur-Oise, declared, when granting *franchises* to the inhabitants of Bonvil'iers, that in wartime he could lead them anywhere where he could lead the inhabitants of the commune of Chambly.

It has been alleged that the particular achievement of the communes was personal freedom, and that the member of the commune was a free man. Let us assume, so as to simplify the argument (though not without hesitation), that freedom in the twelfth or thirteenth centuries was a legal state which was easily definable and identical in all regions of France. In some charters granting a commune, indeed, the abolition of *mortmain* or *chevage* is explicitly stated. But we are justified in thinking that serfdom persisted for a long time, both in communes and free towns. The fact that many communes did not obtain a concession of this kind at the outset, must not be explained merely by the assumption that the serfdom had already come to an end before the granting of a commune. At Senlis, all the inhabitants without exception had to swear to the commune, but there were among their number *hommes de corps* (bondmen) who were obliged to pay their rent on the appointed day or else be fined, and who were forbidden to marry without the lord's consent. The same was true of Soissons, Compiègne and Vailly. On the other hand, by the terms of the customs of certain *villes de franchise*, new inhabitants were regarded as free after a year and a day had elapsed (Lorris charter) or, in some cases, immediately (charters of Méru and Blois). Louis VII abolished *mortmain* at Orléans despite the violent opposition of the royal officers who wished to retain it.

Similarly, charters granting franchises contain articles guaranteeing property, the requirement that a year and a day must elapse before possession of tenure, and rules governing debts and wages. But these charters, whether or not they were granted to a sworn association, are not codes of civil legislation, any more than they are codes of commercial and industrial legislation. Custom is the supreme arbiter in such matters, and the granting of a charter is seen, at the very most, as a chance to reform it or enlarge its scope in one or two respects. There is no question of establishing a new right. The main object of the charter, of whatever type, is to guard the inhabitants against despotic acts. At first sight the best way of achieving this is to be self-governing and to exclude from the town the lord's agents. Here we touch on the vital question. Did the communes enjoy a privilege in this respect? If one is to believe certain historians, the *ville de commune* in the twelfth century differed from the others by having an autonomous administration; indeed, they assert that some of these towns were a kind of republic. This statement must be treated with caution. Scholars who have taken for granted the autonomy of the 'genuine communes' come up against unsurmountable obstacles. Anyone surveying the texts earlier in date than the thirteenth century is obliged to make two preliminary observations. Firstly, the judicial and administrative institutions existing in the twelfth century were not always contemporaneous with the founding of the commune. There are cases when the granting of a commune is merely an addition to ancient municipal franchises, and there is no reason to suppose it was the burgesses' conjuration which obtained those liberties. On the other hand, certain communes, far from enjoying freedoms acquired over the centuries, were sparsely endowed at first; they had to obtain their privileges and guarantees gradually during the twelfth century and, here too, commune and self-government were not achieved at the same time.

When we seek to discover the political and administrative content of the commune charters of the twelfth century, our curiosity is rarely satisfied. What were the powers vested in the general assembly of the inhabitants? It is hardly ever possible to tell. What were the political guarantees enjoyed by the commune? It is occasionally possible to see that certain precautions were taken, for example, the urban class of knights was carefully watched; they were prevented from having a fortified house in the suburbs, or from proclaiming bans in the town; when they had judicial rights, those were redeemed. But nine times out of ten it would be pointless to look in a charter of a commune for a political constitution regulating the number, manner of election, judicial and administrative powers of the municipal magistrates.

The most independent communes were in the northern part of the kingdom. Chief among them was Tournai, with its unique situation "within the confines of the realm, facing the Empire, on the marches of Brabant, Hainault, Cambrésis, Liège", as a letter of Charles VI states in reference to a very ancient state of affairs. All the king wanted was to have on the frontier a fortified town peopled with loyal burgesses, and in any case it would be difficult for his agents to exert any influence over the administration of this enclave. The ancient episcopal *échevinage* was more or less absorbed by the college of ten *jurés* which made all the decisions. The king contented himself with smoothing out the disagreements between bishop and burgesses. So great was his confidence that, in his letters of 1188, Philip Augustus confirmed in advance any Tournai custom he might have neglected to ratify. Judicial independence was complete, with the single exception of the rights enjoyed by the *cour du roi*: the magistrates exercised justice at every level, high, middle and low, in the town and suburbs. In short, Tournai was a kind of burghers' republic.

The political liberties of the commune of Soissons and its group were also wide in scope, but not quite to the same extent: the *jurés* had a considerable share in government, and even had the responsibility for war and peace, should the town become involved in a conflict with a neighbouring lord.

We have no clear picture of the political constitution of Abbeville in the twelfth century. The charter of 1184, which sanctioned existing customs, does little more than tell us the judicial prerogatives of the *échevinage*; in this respect Abbeville was on almost the same level as Tournai. The echevins exercised high justice, took cognizance of theft, attacks and murders, pronounced sentences ranging from demolition of dwellings, physical mutilation and banishment to death. Even so, the property of a thief was confiscated for the benefit of the count of Ponthieu, and it was his delegate, the *vicomte*, who tried civil cases involving a *communier* (a member of a commune) of Abbeville if the case concerned chattels; it was the lord of the land in question who tried the case if it concerned real estate, but the trial took place at Abbeville.

Generally speaking, the legal lords did not act so generously as the counts of Ponthieu did towards Abbeville. They were reluctant to drop fines or to renounce completely the punishment of criminals. For example, the echevins of Arras brought criminal cases, obliged inhabitants who perpetuated family feuds to make a truce or to settle their differences, and they collaborated with the count's law officer (*justicier*) and so received only part of the fines. At Laon, the judicial powers of the mayor and *jurés* were in any case not clearly defined in the charter, and were of only average importance. In almost every case the king, in his communes, retained the administration of higher justice. Giry's study of some ten *échevinages* which coexisted alongside the municipal corporate body even enables us to state that in the earliest period many communes at first possessed only the right of policing and the right to be avenged on those who harmed them. Later, the commune endeavoured, not always successfully, to absorb the old *échevinage* which was left over from the Carolingian *scabinat*. At Noyon, the *échevinage* managed to remain independent up to 1572.

All in all, instead of saying that the communes which did not enjoy complete autonomy were 'demi-communes', it would be better to say that a commune like Tournai was a 'super-commune'. It is scarcely necessary to add that conflicts over jurisdiction were frequent. Agreements in the Middle Ages, even when they were enshrined in a charter, always left room for discussion.

The reason which very often prevented kings from granting the communes very wide autonomy was the income they drew from the towns: Louis VII and Philip Augustus himself hesitated to sell the *prévôté* to the *communiers*; they were afraid of underselling the profit from their domanial lands. They were also afraid of compromising their authority. But the purchase of the royal *prévôté* was the primary condition of the burgesses' independence. It enabled the burgesses to control the exercise of justice and public order and to hold the reins of financial resources which could be increased by rigorous direct administration. There were in the twelfth century some communes which remained *villes de prévôté*, for example Compiègne, Meulan, Mantes, Chaumont-en-Vexin, and Montdidier. When Philip Augustus seized Amiens in 1185 he installed a provost there. In short, historians who designated as *villes de prévôté* those towns which had no commune, used a misleading term. The retention or abolition of the *prévôté* does not constitute a criterion.

The régime of partial autonomy is equally found in seigneurial towns which had obtained a communal charter either from their lord or directly from the king himself. Beauvais had a commune, founded by Louis VI; it still possessed a bishop's provost, and the principle still obtained there that all exercise of justice was the prerogative of the bishop. Dijon still had a provost in the thirteenth century. Similarly Bar-sur-Aube and many other communes also had one. We shall see that, in Dreux, the commune possessed no jurisdiction.

In Normandy and the south of the Loire, the régime of the *Établissements* of Rouen prevailed, which was later granted by the Plantagenets to a great many communes in the Angevin Empire. It was not a very liberal régime. The *Établissements* appear to have been drawn up by order of the king-duke more as a means of codifying citizens' obligations than enumerating their privileges. The inhabitants were obliged to swear fidelity to the commune, otherwise they had to leave the town a year and a day after they had entered it. Anyone presuming to stay without taking the oath was clapped in chains and thrown into prison. Avoidance of military service was punished with extreme severity. There was a penalty ordained for everything, even women's gossip: slanderers and trouble-makers were punished by ducking.

The Hundred Peers, a body from which all three municipal magistrates were drawn, formed a hereditary aristocracy which probably enjoyed the king-duke's favour, and did not genuinely represent the commune as a whole. Together with the twenty-four *jurés* (twelve echevins and twelve councillors), whom they chose from their own number, they were responsible for trying simple cases and for administration. Cases of higher justice were referred to the royal officers; the peers and *jurés* had cognizance of thefts and forgery, "seditions in the town", infringements of the statutes and breach of promise; they intervened to decree that a house be razed to the ground when the legal proceedings *en haute justice* instituted by the royal officers concerned the community as a whole. The municipal officers were severely punished if they neglected their duties or disclosed a secret, and particularly if they accepted bribes. Their personal responsibility was reinforced by a rather ingenious system of assemblies which took place at closer and closer intervals, according to the importance of the position held by each group. Thus, the Hundred met every fortnight, the *jurés* every week and echevins twice a week.

The mayor, elected annually from the town notables, was a most powerful figure. He chaired all the meetings, received the town's revenues, was head of the communal militia and keeper of the keys to the town gates. But he was partially a ducal official, in that the king-duke chose him himself from the list of three candidates submitted by the Peers. This arrangement was destined to gain general acceptance, and by the end of the *Ancien Régime* it was in force in most French towns, which is indicative of the wide guarantees it offered to the sovereign. There can be no doubt that, in the days of Henry II or Richard Lion-Heart, the mayor of Rouen had to serve zealously the interests of those terrible masters. It is, therefore, impossible to speak of a burgesses' republic in the context of a town governed by the *Établissements* of Rouen. It is tempting to think that, whatever restrictions were placed on the autonomy of most of the communes, they were nevertheless more independent than the *villes franches* (free towns). But for this view to be accurate, the *villes franches* would have to be in close subordination to the royal or seigneurial officers. But this was not always the case. They often retained very ancient habits of self-government existing before their charter was granted, or else they had acquired along with their charter considerable privileges in the exercise of justice and government. In Bourges, for example, there still remained a body of *prud'hommes* or *barons*, a relic of an ancient law court in which sat notables, a few knights who lived in the town and the district known as the *septaine de Bourges*, and even clergy living in the town and *septaine*. These *prud'hommes* administered the town under the authority of the royal provost, and the charter of 1181 carefully defined the latter's prerogatives.

The law of Beaumont-en-Argonne, which in the course of four centuries was granted to 500 towns, *villeneuves* and villages, particularly in Champagne, conferred on them administrative and judicial autonomy similar to that of the communes. This law was the achievement of one of the most important figures in the Capet family in the twelfth century, the archbishop of Rheims, William of the White Hands. This great prelate, whom a contemporary styled *secundus rex*, was uncle to Philip Augustus, and acted as regent of France during the Third Crusade. The Beaumont charter, although it was applied in a geographical area extending beyond the actual borders of the kingdom, is a Capetian document. In its original form, that of 1182, it placed the exercise of justice, administration and finance of the town in the hands of a mayor and *jurés*, set up annually with the consent of the inhabitants; they could remain in office provided they had the unanimous consent of the inhabitants. Beaumont and its daughter towns were *villes franches*, which had approximately the same administration, the same jurisdiction, the same general system of law and order as communes which were renowned for the considerable degree of autonomy they enjoyed.

A very clear insight into the policy pursued by William of the White Hands is afforded by his treatment of the inhabitants of Rheims themselves. The case of this archiepiscopal town should have given pause to those historians who persist in trying to discover which, in the twelfth century, were the institutions specific to the communes. The commune charter, together with the concession of the liberties of Laon which Louis VII had granted to the inhabitants of Rheims, had been revoked by him in

1130 at the request of the clergy; the court of echevins was allowed to continue. The king's brother Henry, who became archbishop of Rheims in 1160, suppressed this court. In 1182, William of the White Hands, who succeeded Henry, restored to the burgesses of Rheims "within his ban" the customs which, to quote the royal chancery, "had been granted them in former days, and for some years had not been properly preserved because of a change of lord", and he "restored the echevins to the city". The burgesses obtained twelve echevins elected by them to exercise justice. But they were still denied the privilege of a commune, and the act of 1182, the so-called *charte wilhelmine*, remained the charter of the city of Rheims, a free town (*ville franche*) without a commune, possessing all the liberties which it had been granted when it was a commune. It is, therefore, certain that a commune and an autonomous municipality meant two completely separate things to the men of the twelfth century. Archbishop William had no desire to have a commune in his town, because, like many clergy, he was afraid of organized resistance; he regarded the form of the sworn association as constituting a danger. But he was quite prepared to leave the task of administration and the exercise of justice to the elected representatives of the inhabitants.

Let us compare the *charte wilhelmine*, a charter granting a franchise, with a contemporary document, the commune charter granted two years previously by Robert II, count of Dreux, fourth son of Louis VI, to the burgesses of Dreux. These people had formed a commune in the days of Louis VI, but had no charter. If we interpret the text correctly, this fact provoked bickering between factions in the town, or at any rate violent disagreement with the count. The count in question, we are told by the historian of the house of Dreux, "was easy-going, placid and peace-loving", and he gave proof of this by concluding agreements with the lords who disputed with him. He also made an agreement with the burgesses of Dreux, and his act illustrates everything we have just said about charters granting a commune and charters granting franchises. We cannot do better than give a complete translation of it. It will show how modest, in some cases, were the privileges accompanying the granting of a commune:

In the name of the holy and indivisible Trinity, Amen.

Since, among other deficiencies of human frailty, we are subject to loss and lapse of memory, divine Providence decreed, to compensate for this inconvenience, the invention of durable writing, so that the permanent characters may preserve unchanged that which at every moment is subject to change, by reason of the frequent variations of things. Bearing in mind the permanence of writing, I, Robert, by the longsuffering of God count of Dreux and Braine, brother of Louis the illustrious king of France, wish, by these written characters, to inform all, present and future, that a disagreement having arisen between me and my burgesses of Dreux, we finally decided on this agreement, namely, we allowed them to have the commune they had in my father's day, and we confirmed it to them by oath, I, Agnes countess of Braine my wife, and Robert my son. Moreover (*etiam*) we swore to the aforesaid burgesses that we would not levy, nor would our successors levy, any *tolte* or *taille* on the aforesaid burgesses and we would do them no violence. But we will put an end to all their strife by giving them peace if this can be done. If their disagreement, whatever it is, cannot be resolved by a peace, we shall put an end to it in our court by the judgement of wise men and our loyal subjects. They themselves have sworn to be loyal to me, to my wife and heirs and to guard and defend our fortified town of Dreux against all comers; to confirm and not to cede our rights and just customs and judgements, and this at all times and in all places; not to oppose them, but rather, if need be, to cause them to be respected as best they may. We have moreover given an undertaking to these same burgesses not to force anyone from their commune to use our mills or to pay other dues. We have limited our *banvin* to one month between Christmas and the beginning of Quadragesima and to another month between Easter and the Nativity of St John the Baptist; we shall not buy wine to resell it because of our ban, and we have agreed that the impost of one-third on the retail sale of drinks shall not be levied. In addition, each time I and my heirs have to do military service for the king, they will provide me and my heirs with three waggons and three horses harnessed to them, at my expense after they leave the town. At no other time shall I have the power to oblige the burgesses to hand over to me or lend me either waggons or horses. But if they so wish, either because I request them or because of the love they bear me, they may lend me their own horses and waggons. As is due and proper, the aforesaid burgesses shall be obliged to use my wine presses. To ensure that all these agreements persist in a permanent and stable form, I have decided to lend them the weight of the signatures of witnesses and to affix my seal. Done publicly at Sens, the year of the incarnation of the Word 1180, Philip being king in France, Alexander being pope, Guy being archbishop of Sens, and John bishop of Chartres. Given by the hand of the clerk Bernard.

The signatures are those of Peter de Courtenay, Count Robert's brother, and of thirteen others. Thus the town of Dreux, one of the most ancient communes in France, was granted, rather late in the day, a charter which entailed no political liberty. Many other communes, whose charters have not come down to us, certainly likewise had no 'wide prerogative'. The burgesses of Dreux had neither administrative autonomy nor judicial prerogatives (*droits de justice*). The count merely promised them paternal government which would settle their differences, would eschew all violence and extortion, and would not oblige the inhabitants to wage war in the service of the king of France. He sanctioned the old sworn association probably because it seemed to him a pledge of concord, of fraternal unity under his aegis. By contrast with the archbishop of Rheims, he did not regard the "conjuration" of the burgesses as a threat to his authority; for him, as indeed for many lords of his day, it was a "peaceful institution".

The history of Dreux is a typical example of a situation which cautions us against the danger of complex definitions which do not occur in the texts; these provide a simple definition which is universally applicable.

3. Role of the commune in urban emancipation. Example of Saint-Quentin

Does this mean that we must deny that the communal movement played a leading part in the great municipal revolution of the twelfth century? We must dismiss such an idea. We have seen that it is impossible to state that the communal movement was the first act of the drama of urban emancipation. But it did speed the action. In the twelfth century, as the communes gained ground, the burgesses of other towns obtained political liberties which they had not dared to claim at first. The Beaumont charter and the *charte wilhelmine* were granted at the end of the period studied in this chapter. It was not until the reign of Philip Augustus that charters of free towns increased in number, with the emergence of elected magistrates: echevins, peers, etc. The communal movement was a leaven which gradually permeated the mass of burgesses. The fact that in certain towns the inhabitants bound themselves together by oath and succeeded in having this oath treated as valid by their lord was of the utmost importance. These *communiers* felt – and were felt to be – emboldened by these solemn commitments. Not only were they able, generally speaking, to maintain their freedoms, but they also widened their scope. In many cases municipal autonomy was arrived at by means of a slow progression which sometimes suffered setbacks. The communes were examples of an unremitting effort to attain this autonomy.

One wishes it were possible, in every case, to be familiar with this spread of urban liberties and to discern, instead of a static condition, an evolutionary movement, born of the energy of the commune members. Detailed study of these vicissitudes is not often possible, in view of the large-scale disappearance of the documents which would throw light on them. It would be pointless to try to discover in detail the constitutional history of a free town like Orleans or a short-lived commune like Étampes. But there are one or two towns whose history can, despite gaps in the original sources, be safely scrutinized. Saint-Quentin is one of these.

Let us examine in detail the charter granted to the inhabitants of Saint-Quentin by Philip Augustus in 1195, which reproduces (probably in full, with some additions) the charter granted some years earlier by the Countess Eleanor, of which only the opening clauses remain, and which probably represent the first third of the charter. According to this document, the population of Saint-Quentin included, on the one hand, burgesses bound by the communal oath, and on the other knights and vavasours, together with sergeants, who were not part of the commune; there was also a body of clergy whose most eminent members were the dean and canons of the church. The interrelations of these various categories of inhabitant are defined with some accuracy in certain spheres, and do not appear to have generated friction at the time when the charter was drawn up.

Admission to the commune of Saint-Quentin was governed by rules which are quite clearly set forth. For instance, men from the countess' domain and, in Philip Augustus' charter, men of the king's bodyguard are not admitted. But the king's freemen are allowed to be members of the commune and men owing allegiance to other lords are also allowed to join. Once they are part of the commune, the new burgesses may enjoy freedom of person and property and may also keep, without fear of molestation, everything they bring with them. They may also keep their real estate, but any chattels they leave behind will become the property of their former lord. The burgesses are dispensed from all mortmain. Once you are a member of the commune you must take up residence there, except when called away by business (*negocia*). As a great many burgesses have plots of land in the country, they can take protracted holidays, from the Purification of the Virgin until the end of April "for their March", and from the Nativity of St John the Baptist to Martinmas "for their August".

The greater part of the charter concerns the exercise of justice. As regards the cases falling under the ecclesiastical jurisdiction, the burgesses respond only to the writ of summons of the dean sitting in chapter; any improper summons would provoke the protective intervention of the king. The three kinds of lay justice are:

(1) The count's court, composed of the free men of the 'honour' or *seigneurie* of Saint-Quentin, the knights, and the clergy or their representatives. It tries the cases brought by the count against the commune. If one of the parties overturns the verdict, recourse is had to a judicial duel.

(2) The tribunal of echevins. One is bound to accept Giry's account of the origins of the *échevinage* of Saint-Quentin. It is the ancient Carolingian *scabinat*, the law-court trying on behalf of the lord almost all

civil and criminal cases. There is no conflict between the *échevinage* and the commune, indeed, the burgesses regard it as a privilege to be tried by the *échevinage*. Even so they do have an influence and, from 1215, exert direct control over the choice of echevins. The castellan or *vicomte*, the count's representative in the town, co-operates with the echevins and the population in keeping order and punishing the guilty. Crimes committed within the town or committed against someone leaving the town attract, as may be readily believed, capital punishment if the perpetrators of these crimes have caused death. "Justice will be meted out to him as if he has committed murder." In the case of a wounding, or if the murderer has escaped, the penalty is banishment. In all these cases the guilty party's house is destroyed and his property confiscated. The sentence is less severe if the attack against the person is the result of a long-standing hatred, a feud: if a burgess, who is out of town on business, is killed "in a mortal feud", the murderer is not deemed to deserve banishment in perpetuity. In such a case, obviously, steps were taken to create a "peace" between the two families. The count reserves the right to prosecute the inhabitants of the commune before the echevins for cases of murder, theft, abduction, arson, and other cases of higher justice (*nostra sunt*) in which the accused and his property belong to him absolutely. But the burgesses may take it upon themselves to arrest a thief; they will be relieved of all responsibility as soon as they have handed him over to the castellan; he will first set the thief in the pillory and then try him with the help of the echevins.

(3) The mayor and *jurés* of Saint-Quentin are responsible, as far as the outer suburbs, for administering justice and maintaining public order, and their functions sometimes overlap those exercised by the *échevinage*. Provided their sentence has been fair and reasonable, no one may appeal against it. *Ratione persone*, they alone exercise jurisdiction over the sergeants of the commune and the keepers of the town gates, in all matters relating to chattels. *Ratione materie*, they can possess heirs of their rights without waiting for possible law-suits to be brought before the competent legal authorities. If a purchaser refuses to pay cash, the vendor may ask the mayor to oblige him to do so. The same course is open to a workman employed by a burgess who refuses to pay his wages. The mayor and *jurés* do not merely fulfil the role of justices of the peace. They also have cognizance of heinous crimes committed against the commune, and in such cases they have the right to pronounce the sentence of banishment and order the offender's house to be pulled down. But they can also deal with offences brought before them in the hope that they will increase the penalties decreed by the echevins. On these occasions they can

pronounce a sentence of banishment; if the accused has a house, they can order its demolition, or they can impose a heavy fine. We gather from another article that they can banish thieves. Banishment and the pulling down of a house were fearful punishments. If the house was fortified the count came and helped them pull it down. If the exiles attempted to return, they were shown no mercy: the mayor and *jurés* "wrought their vengeance on them just as they pleased".

The burgess secured guarantees against possible abuses. This charter reveals the kind of harassments and acts of violence from which it protects him. His natural judges, whether lay or ecclesiastical, cannot summon him to appear in court outside Saint-Quentin. Furthermore, when he has left the town, a creditor, a fellow-member of the commune, cannot claim what is owed to him; the burgess cannot be summoned by another judicial body except inside a fortified place (*castellum*). In the countryside, where he would no doubt be exposed to acts of violence, he is only legally liable for the payment of his dues. If, at Saint-Quentin, anyone wishes to serve a summons on a burgess it must not be at night, or when he leaves home to attend an assembly at the mayor's house, or an assembly summoned by the bell, or when he has to join the militia. If he is arrested, his wife must not be arrested also, and his clothes cannot be removed. He cannot be taken outside the town or brutally treated; he can be put in chains with his feet tied together, but that is all. The king may not summon a member of the commune to judicial combat; a burgess may compel a man to engage in a legal duel, but the champion must be a member of the commune. In other words, the old usage of the judicial combat is maintained, but the professional champion is not countenanced and the king cannot initiate this kind of contest.

Certain remedies are available to put pressure on insolvents who are not members of the commune. A creditor who meets a debtor from another town in Saint-Quentin may apprehend him and use force if need be, until the law intervenes. There are sergeants and vavasours living in the town who owe allegiance to no lord and who do not fall under the echevins' jurisdiction; if they are unwilling to pay a debt, they are obliged to find a lord, within a fortnight, who will try the case and also may have recourse to judicial combat, with certain safeguards. Should he refuse, the echevins are competent to try the case.

Other articles settle questions of loan against security, protect minors who need not appear before the courts so long as they earn no money, and forbid a wife to stand bail except when her husband is away and she is also engaged in trade. Lastly, possession of tenure is assured after a year and a day have elapsed.

As is almost always the case in charters granting a commune, the clauses of an administrative or political nature are scanty and only half-satisfy our curiosity. However, they do show us that Saint-Quentin was one of the Capetian communes which enjoyed fairly wide autonomy. There was no provost and the municipality controlled the town's resources. The king, who was paid a fixed sum in dues, refrained from levying any taxes, and possessed neither mills nor ovens. The burgesses were free to mill their flour and bake their bread wherever they wished. If the mayor and *jurés* were short of money for the running of the town they were empowered, provided the community of burgesses agreed, to levy imposts on the capital and landed property of these burgesses, and on all the money earned in the town, and to impose fines on those who refused to pay. The Saint-Quentin charter shows that they spent the money raised by taxes on wheeled traffic on the upkeep of the public highway, while the income from certain types of fine was spent on fortifications. The mayor and *jurés* were responsible for the defence of the town and erected fortifications wherever they thought fit. They had not the right to mint money, but their consent was needed for any change of coinage.

The clause dealing with military service owed to the king implies unlimited obligation. "Every time we convene the commune", says Philip Augustus, "the commune will rally to our banners." I see in this imperious clause an addition ordered by Philip Augustus. His charter bears witness to his good will in granting considerable autonomy to the burgesses of Saint-Quentin, provided they maintained in their town order and good justice and that their town, of vital importance in the defence of the kingdom, was well fortified and well guarded.

At this point the question arises: to what extent do Countess Eleanor's mutilated charter and Philip Augustus' charter set before us the original liberties of Saint-Quentin?

The ancient settlement of Augusta Viromandorum which had grown up around the basilica of Saint-Quentin and had taken the apostle's name, is probably, if one discounts the abortive attempt made by Le Mans, the oldest commune in France. Cambrai, an even older commune, was in the territory of the Holy Roman Empire. The insurrection of the inhabitants of Cambrai against their bishop took place in 1076; Cambrai was one day's journey away from Saint-Quentin. At this time the count of Vermandois, Herbert IV (1045–1080), was the lord of Saint-Quentin, as the husband of Adèle de Valois. It was undoubtedly he who, in the closing years of his reign, permitted the burgesses of this town to form a commune. The only available information on this matter is contained in the preambles to the charters subsequently granted by Countess Eleanor and King Philip Augustus.

When the commune was first granted, all the principal peers of Vermandois and all the clergy, saving the rights of the clergy, and all the knights, saving the fealty due to the count, swore to uphold it steadfastly. The commune was established in such a way that the members of the commune remained completely free and in full possession of their property; neither we nor any other may prosecute a member of the commune except by means of trial by the echevins, nor may we claim mortmain from a member of the commune.

There is no good reason to suppose that any other promises were made by Count Herbert IV, for no charter granted by him has come down to us and there is no mention by anyone in the twelfth century of a document of this kind.

The first century of the history of the commune of Saint-Quentin is obscure. We have no direct information on its development in the time of Hugh the Great, Raoul I, Raoul II and Philip of Alsace, count of Flanders, who married the heiress of Vermandois, Elisabeth. On her death on 26 March 1182, the title was to pass to her sister Eleanor, wife of Matthew III, count of Beaumont-sur-Oise. Eleanor of Beaumont disputed its possession with Philip of Alsace. When he died on 1 June 1191 she finally acquired the Vermandois and Saint-Quentin. It was clearly at this juncture that she granted the charter, a few fragments of which remain. She lived on until June 1213, but in the winter of 1191–92 she had signed a convention with Philip Augustus placing her under the king's patronage; Philip was to enter into possession of Saint-Quentin if she should die childless. In 1195 he saw fit to confirm Countess Eleanor's charter and promised to uphold the usages and customs of Saint-Quentin when the town came under his control. The point at issue, according to the preamble to the two charters, was "the usages and customs which the burgesses of Saint-Quentin held in the time of Count Raoul and his ancestors".

The simplest assumption would be that Saint-Quentin had not ceased, ever since the foundation of the commune, to enjoy the liberties originally granted by Herbert IV, and that these liberties are described in the charters granted by Eleanor and Philip Augustus. But, as I stated above, no charter is in existence from Count Herbert's hand and the concessions attributed to him by the preambles to the charters of 1191 and 1195 are very limited. Moreover, we do possess an intermediate document which in my opinion makes such an assumption impossible. This is a long unofficial report, the *Établissements* of Saint-Quentin, sent by the burgesses of the town to the inhabitants of Eu, in about 1151, obviously in response to a request for information. One would expect to find the clauses of Eleanor's charter and the king's charter, with commentaries, but this is certainly not the case. The texts of the *Établissements* and of the charters granted forty years later are different. It is true that the preamble to the *Établissements* and the articles they contain are more or less the same. These relate to the burgesses' property which must be respected, the burgess who has arrested a thief and handed him over to the law, the bestowal of property belonging to new burgesses, the burgesses' right not to have a summons served on them when outside the town, and holidays granted for work on the land, together with the lord's promise not to levy a tax (Arts. 3, 18, 28, 34, 35, 46). Apart from these exceptions, the fifty-four articles of Eleanor's and the king's charters are not paralleled in the fifty-three articles of the *Établissements*. Not only do the *Établissements* begin by the commune oath, which is not found in the charters ("All swore common aid to their *juré*, and common counsel and common property and common defence", Art. 2), but they present us with municipal institutions which are not at the same stage of development as the institutions recognized by Philip Augustus, and the former, though composed at an earlier date, are surprisingly more liberal than the latter. In the *Établissements*, entry into the commune is much easier: "The gate is open to all" (Art. 28): "whoever wishes to, no matter whence he comes, provided he is not a thief, may live in the commune, and as soon as he has entered the town, no-one may lay a finger on him or offer him violence" (Art. 4). The considerable reservations of the 1195 charter are not evident here. In addition, no one may live in the town without the permission of the mayor and echevins (Art. 49) and, furthermore, once a man is received into the commune and then attempts unjustifiably, through motives of anger or disdain, to opt out, his house will be pulled down and he may even be proscribed for ever (Art. 30). The gates which stand wide open without any apparent concern for other people, close with exceptional severity on those who enter them.

The most striking difference between the *Établissements* of Saint-Quentin and the charters is that the judicial rights of the commune are much wider in the earlier document. The castellan or viscount, whose powers were redefined at the end of the century by the king of France, have forfeited many of their prerogatives to the mayor. It seems that the echevins who earlier formed a seigneurial law-court have become his collaborators. Time and again they are mentioned side by side. The echevins become the mouthpiece of the commune and it is the commune which has, in actual fact, legal sovereignty. The principle advanced, which is in any case too absolute not to be at variance with certain clauses, is that "common justice is binding on and is applicable to burgesses, knights, and everyone down to the very lowest" and that "this commune is ultimately responsible for administering justice to all".

If an inhabitant is assaulted, if his clothes are torn and his face scarred with deep scratches, "the mayor of the commune will see that he is avenged" and the guilty party will be more harshly treated "if he is in the habit of doing such things" (Art. 16). If a *juré* is beaten or unjustly despoiled of his property, the guilty party "powerful or not powerful" will not be able to enter the town before he has "admitted before the *jurés* to having inflicted the damage and committed the crime, and restored what he has taken; otherwise, if he does enter Saint-Quentin, "it might happen by chance that he would suffer death or some other act of cruelty because of it". Moreover, if he is caught, "the mayor, if he sees fit, may cut off one of his limbs, or deal with him in some other way", and shall not be molested for so doing (Art. 33). When a still more serious crime has taken place in the town, it is not the castellan or viscount, the count's justiciary, who will deal with the matter, as was the case in former times, and as is laid down in a subsequent charter of 1195. If a serious wound has been inflicted the guilty party shall have his fist cut off: if the wound is slight, he will be driven out of town, if the commune so decides. If death has been caused, the murderer's house is to be pulled down and he will be handed over to be "tried by the mayor and the echevins or banished in perpetuity, or mutilated before being banished, and his property destroyed", he will even be "treated with greater severity according to the gravity of the offence and the extent to which the town would benefit by such a course" (Arts. 17 and 47). If there is a feud, and an inhabitant is prosecuted outside the town "for a long-standing hatred" and if the accused refuses to clear himself on oath in the presence of the mayor, his house will be pulled down, and "if it pleases the legal officers of the commune", his hand will be cut off and he will be banished for as long as the commune wishes (Art. 13).

Crimes against the commune itself are, of course, punished by it. "If we catch a man stealing our commune's property, then we may wreak our vengeance on him without any other legal formality" (Art. 37). And if any man, powerful or not, incites his fellows to despise or hate the commune and seeks to destroy it, and if this can be proved either by two or three witnesses or in any other way, it would be better for that man not to enter the town or fall into the commune's power, for he may well have a limb cut off, or his house pulled down, or all his property destroyed (Art. 40).

The men who drafted the *Établissements* are obliged to acknowledge the existence of justice administered by the count, but if one of the count's officers attempts to try a case "by illegal methods", the mayor "will bid him judge equitably, and if he refuses to do so, the mayor can then try the case according to the law" (Art. 32). In short, in so far as any clear conclusions can be drawn from a muddled, prolix text which exists only in a bad translation, it seems that the mayor concerns himself with all the cases which do not impinge on the count's personal interests.

The *Établissements* are curiously aggressive in tone. It is obvious that the authors are 'democratic' burgesses, fiercely attached to the rights they have arrogated to themselves. They say, for example, that no one is obliged to appear in court if summoned by a lawyer if the count and *jurés* take no interest in the case (Art. 10). No one has the right to challenge anyone to combat (Art. 6). The clergy alone are safe from threats and bitterness. Even the echevins and the mayor are themselves not above suspicion and keep their eye on each other. If an echevin succumbs to corruption, the *jurés* of the commune can decide to pull his house down "or do justice in some other way"; if it is the mayor who has "taken a bribe" the echevins' justice will pull down his house and may demote him (Art. 27). If a burgess, taken to court by the mayor's or count's justice, is called to stand trial in camera, and if he is injured when a door is slammed in his face (this must be a reminiscence of an actual incident of this kind), the mayor runs the risk of having his hand cut off, his house pulled down, and being "driven out of the town in perpetuity" (Art. 9). The mayor and echevins are forbidden when "attacking a fortress on military service" to strike a member of the commune (Art. 38).

An even more conspicuous feature of the document is the haughty and provocative attitude it displays towards the lord of the town, the neighbouring lords, and the knights of Saint-Quentin, who are freely referred to as "rascally lords governed by greed" (Art. 42), and are perpetually threatened and under suspicion. The knights of Saint-Quentin, who had originally sworn to uphold the commune and were not members of it, are taken to task in a tone both protective and suspicious. No objection is made to their living in the country, but these country noblemen must rush to bear arms at once should their support ever be needed to ward off danger; if their lords dare to deflect them from their military duties "the power of the commune would wreak vengeance on them and would pull down these lords' houses if the mayor so wished" (Art. 26). These local noblemen, these Vermandois peers who also swore to uphold the commune when it was formed, were under close surveillance. Within a perimeter of three leagues around the town, they are not allowed to have a fortified dwelling (Art. 7). They may not deny a just trial to their knights, they must not rob their own men or strangers in the town, realize fraudulent profits in currency deals or contract debts without offering sound pledges and stating the terms of the deal (Arts. 22, 29, 35, 41–43). They have no right to place any obstacle in the way of building houses or adding another storey to them. They may not deny justice to the members of the commune when these request to be tried by them (Art. 29).

The count does not enjoy a much greater degree of trust. Like the other nobles, he may not "cry shame and dishonour (*vilenie*) on a burgess" nor incite his sergeants to acts of violence (Art. 12). He may only enter the town if he has a small escort of four or twelve knights (Art. 44). If he has a fortified house there, he may use as guards only members of the commune who have been accepted by the mayor and *jurés*, and not people "who wish the destruction of the burgesses" (Art. 31). If he brings in and establishes in the town knights or sergeants at arms who are unauthorized and armed, they will be thrown out (Art. 44). When he requires military service, those serving must be able to return home the same day: if a man agrees "at his request and to his great advantage" to do more, this should not become a habit (Art. 7). If he needs money, a burgess may give him some of his own free will, but no help is owed him, nor is any ditch-digging corvée owed him (Art 8). Even the amount of bread, meat and wine he may be supplied with on credit is specified, "and we shall have the discretion to offer him further credit". Provision is made for his defaulting on his debts: the community will reimburse his creditor (Art. 36). The peace of the market is guaranteed by the commune, obviously against the prince's officers; lawbreakers will run the risk of having a hand cut off, their house pulled down, and even "other penalties" (Art. 5). The count's officers may not, to assert their authority, take advantage of quarrels breaking out amongst the burgesses during a war or on feast days or assembly days, nor may they use as a pretext the words a burgess may let slip in the courtroom "after dinner" (Arts. 14–15, 19).

In short, the *Établissements* of Saint-Quentin reveal to us a set of impatient, acrimonious, excitable burgesses, quick to utter threats and probably to behave impulsively; people who have no intention of being led and often try to lead other people; who mistrust the count, the "powerful or non-powerful", the local nobility, the knights of the town and environs, the count's officers and even the echevins and mayor. It is surprising that the men who drafted the account of this consultation requested by the burgesses of Eu did not, in 1151, invoke an original charter, only the attitudes adopted by the members of the association on the strength of their oath, the customs to which they firmly adhered and the additions they had made to them. Formulae such as these recur a score of times: "It is confirmed by oath . . ." (Arts. 3, 5) or "we have sworn that . . ." (Art. 7); "it is something sacred and a custom of our commune that . . ." (Art. 9); "after this, we added to the above-mentioned matters . . ." (Art. 23); "we also established it as a custom that . . ." (Art. 25); "we also established by means of an oath that . . ." (Art. 27); "we deemed that . . ." (Art. 33); and other similar formulae.

I can see only one possible explanation, namely that the usages and customs attributed by Countess Eleanor and King Philip to the time of the two counts Raoul and their ancestors had been handed down either by means of a separate charter, or by oral tradition, and that this had failed to satisfy the burgesses. They had accordingly introduced additions and modifications which they had sanctioned by decisions of their general assembly and by oaths. What we know of the history of the Vermandois in the twelfth century enables us to understand what happened, provided we take the usual precaution of relating the facts to our general historical awareness.

At no time during this period did Saint-Quentin have a count governing the country wisely, moderately and firmly. Sometimes the count was absent or inefficient; sometimes he attempted to quash the liberties granted by Herbert IV. Herbert's son-in-law, Hugh the Great, son of King Henry I who succeeded his father-in-law (1080–1102), took part in the First Crusade and made another trip to the Holy Land in 1102, where he died. His son Raoul I (1102–1152) was one of the great figures of the twelfth century. He was seneschal to Louis VI and Louis VII, namely viceroy, and he married Queen Eleanor's sister. He was often seen sitting in court passing sentence, he led expeditions in the service of the king of France, to whom he seems to have been a loyal aide; in 1147, during the Second Crusade, he was joint regent with Abbot Suger of Saint-Denis. Consequently, he spent much of his career outside the Vermandois. His son Raoul II (1152–1163?) was only a leprous child at this time, so the Vermandois was attacked by the neighbouring lords. In the course of the troubled years which followed the powerful count of Flanders, Philip of Alsace, son-in-law to Raoul I, gained possession of the Vermandois.

It is not difficult to surmise that in the reigns of Hugh the Great and Raoul I, who were scarcely ever at home, the burgesses of Saint-Quentin were able to add to the customs and privileges with which Herbert IV had endowed them. Their municipal life was stormy: they obviously had disagreements with the local nobles, and their relations with Raoul I, when he did come to the Vermandois, must have been difficult; for a contemporary chronicler, Lambert of Watrelos, canon of Cambrai, tells us he was a man "of unparalleled greed" and we know, too, that he had a violent character. He probably insisted on a garrison at Saint-Quentin, exacted money to maintain his rank as seneschal, and minted bad currency. He may also have sold privileges. In young Raoul II's reign the town's autonomy could not but increase. Then came a violent reaction during the reign of Philip of Alsace.

Indeed, we are told by the prior of Marchiennes that "in the year of Our Lord 1179 the count of Flanders Philip of Alsace laid waste Saint-Quentin and Péronne and deeply humiliated their inhabitants by a siege and a long persecution". Giry quoted this text *en passant*; Emmanuel Lemaire also reproduced it and concluded that the inhabitants of Saint-Quentin had reached the stage of "thinking they were quite independent", that they failed to recognize the authority of Philip of Alsace, and that he quashed their commune. I do not think it is possible to understand exactly what happened without setting these facts against the general history of the reign of Philip of Alsace.

Vanderkindere showed that the earlier historians of Belgium had painted the municipal politics of the Alsace dynasty in false colours. This dynasty had attained power at a time when the weakening of the authority of the counts, together with civil war precipitated by the assassination of Count Charles the Good in 1127, had emboldened the burgesses and encouraged them to obtain security and prosperity by their own exertions, that is, by modifying the practice of established institutions. The tribunal of echevins, from being a seigneurial court, gradually became the organ of a 'free' burgess class. In 1138, Thierry of Alsace had to give up the attempt to reduce the rebellious town of Ghent. When his pocket was threatened he proved more persistent: he refused to let the town of Thérouanne deprive him of his rent and toll and in 1150 he concluded an agreement with Bishop Milo in order to keep the commune under control. But on the whole he proved easy-going and readily granted privileges, so that the great industrial towns continued their progress towards autonomy.

After him, Philip of Alsace fell prey to anxiety and initiated the reactionary policy later to be pursued so harshly by the dukes of Burgundy. Particularly after his return from the Holy Land in 1178, he blocked the advance of the *villes de loi* and set about putting an end to the communal system. The five famous charters with which he settled the fate of Arras, Ypres, Ghent, Bruges and Oudenarde, and the 1178 ordonnance, mark a retreat. The communal oath with its promise of mutual help, and the guarantees of individual liberty disappeared. The fine for serious crimes was raised to the enormous figure of sixty livres; the administration of the town and the exercise of justice were concentrated in the hands of the echevins, who became once more the count's agents and were chosen by him, *electione principis et non aliter.* It was in this repressive atmosphere that the towns of Artois and Vermandois existed for some years. Clearly, they shared the fate of the Flemish towns. Just as Ghent was punished and threatened with the building of a massive castle for the count, just as the Hesdin commune was abolished, and the *amitié* of Aire-sur-Lys (as the commune was called) was deprived of its bell, the symbol of civic solidarity, so at last Saint-Quentin and Péronne were punished, probably by a reorganization of their administration and judicial system.

After the death of Philip of Alsace, Eleanor of Vermandois was evidently requested to give the towns back their liberties. I would point out that at the same time, about 1192, Countess Matilda, widow of Philip of Alsace, who had to defend herself against the claims of Baldwin of Hainault, restored to the people of Ghent some of their franchises and granted them a tribunal of echevins chosen by co-optation. Eleanor of Vermandois was obliged to do the same; but her charter, and subsequently Philip Augustus' charter, were compromises. Saint-Quentin never regained the very considerable franchises the inhabitants had won during the twelfth century and which were reflected in the *Établissements* communicated to the town of Eu. Its history in the twelfth century, as far as it can be guessed at, is most instructive. The steps towards the emancipation of the town were due to the repeated efforts of the burgesses; the setbacks were caused by the lord's resistance; this was to be expected. Nor should one make the mistake of supposing that the granting of a commune implied the concession of far-ranging liberties immediately agreed to by the lord.

The reader may guess my conclusion: it is certain that the granting of a commune was, originally, in no way linked with any given administrative or judicial institution. If such a link occasionally existed, it may be supposed that in most cases the town maintained or restored old customs. But the communal association, in the 150 years which constitute its young, active period, had a strength and a dynamism which generated progress. The institutions of the communal town evolved, not because the lord desired change, but because the burgesses did. We have seen how, in Saint-Quentin, they extended their privileges and their scope of activity, constantly forged ahead, removed the count's representative from their municipal affairs, and fashioned the body of echevins into an organ which collaborated with the mayor. In so doing, the burgesses in the communes provoked a general movement towards urban emancipation, and the towns which could not obtain a commune did at least, very often, win guarantees, often similar to the guarantees with which certain communes had to be satisfied. The most fortunate of the free towns were as richly endowed as those communes which had been unable to shake off the lord's or the king's *prévôté* and were subject to administrative and financial tutelage.

In the twelfth century, the original feature which gave the commune its distinctive character and which was never lost sight of, was the burgesses' conjuration, the oath of mutual aid, which was fittingly called the *communia*.

CHAPTER 3

Why the communes were granted. The political value of the commune in the kingdom. Evolution of this concept in the twelfth century

1. Established historical facts. Variable attitude of the princes

I have shown, in the foregoing chapters, that the only distinctive feature of the granting of a commune was the permission to form a sworn association. I shall now attempt to discover why the lords and kings of France made this concession and on what conditions it was deemed necessary by the inhabitants or by the lord or by both at once; it will be seen that there were cases in which the idea of a commune had occurred to the lord alone, without the inhabitants appearing to ask for it, or indeed desire it.

Historians have described the very diverse attitudes of ecclesiastical and secular princes to the communal movement. It is well known that the Church, which administered its domains with great care, regarded these conjurations as a challenge to their rights, and put up a long and tenacious resistance to them; whereas the lords and kings were from the outset less rigid: the lure of a large sum of money offered by the burgesses, or else a desire to compete with some ecclesiastical power or other, may have been the motive for their concessions. Louis VI and Louis VII pursued a vacillating policy, determined more by expediency than by any overall grasp of the situation; Philip Augustus and Louis VIII were the first and the last of the French kings to favour the creation of communes in a systematic way.

There is nothing new in all this. My only reason for returning to the subject is to expand and occasionally modify other accounts, some of which are justly famous. I shall take up the tragic story of the Laon commune because it has not yet been related accurately enough. But my main task will be to emphasize a point which has not been made sufficiently clear: those granting the charters were concerned not merely with the resultant advantages in the form of revenue to fill their empty coffers, or a means of weakening a neighbouring lord. They were often aware of the services which might be rendered by sworn associations of burgesses. Right from the start there were some, even clergy (a point I shall insist on), who realized that the communal oath was an element of public order. Subsequently, in the second half of the twelfth century, the kings perceived that it was also a 'national' guarantee – if I may be allowed such an anachronism – a means of resisting the enemies of the realm. As a result, a 'feudal' aspect of the communes became more pronounced; this has long ago been noticed, but it needs to be set out exactly.

2. *Institutio pacis*

In the eleventh century brigandage was the worst obstacle in the way of the revival of economic prosperity and civilized life. A king such as Philip I, even one or two bishops, and probably the majority of the secular nobility, regarded it as a necessary and normal phenomenon. Inside the towns, the merchants and artisans were tyrannized, and sometimes formed rival factions; there was little or no civic authority to put down riots or prevent local inhabitants and outsiders from coming to blows. Outside the town gates life was even less secure; it even happened that peasants who lived on the outskirts of the town, people who were often subsequently included in the commune, were subjected to the brutality and plundering of the townspeople. Pirenne has shown convincingly that one of the reasons for urban emancipation was the need for peace and security felt by the working population.

I shall begin by relating the history of a commune founded by violence, abolished by a contrary act of force and reconstituted by an agreement between the disputants: the Laon commune. It is a typical story, rendered more interesting by the existence of one of those rare detailed accounts by an eye-witness, Guibert, abbot of Nogent-sous-Coucy. He is, let it be said, a prejudiced witness. He was a scornful, angry opponent of the communal movement, and his account is most confused. But there exists as a corrective the more circumstantial 1128 charter from which may be deduced the burgesses' just grounds for complaint, and some further details, about the sequel of the insurrection, are supplied by Suger and Hermann, a monk at Laon.

The old Carolingian walled town of Laon, perched on a hill overlooking the vines and farmland, seemed perfectly placed to guarantee the safety of its inhabitants. Two powerful lords who could have protected them, the bishop and the king of France, shared the comital powers between them. But in fact, in the eleventh century and the beginning of the twelfth, Laon was rent by strife. The clergy and the knights, linked by family ties, were in league to oppress and exploit the tradesmen, artisans and wine-growers living in the town, many of whom were in any case still subject to the burdens of serfdom. What kind of people were these commoners who were about to effect the most bloody of any communal revolution known in France? Guibert assures us that some of them also practised brigandage and harassed the peasants who dared to come to market. This is probably a generalization from a few exceptional cases. However, the burgesses of Laon were undoubtedly exasperated by the exactions of the powerful and by the troubles they caused them. Dowries, marriage settlements and inheritances were frequently snatched away from those entitled to them. Vendettas were pursued without the victims' families obtaining the customary satisfactions. There was no municipal jurisdiction, and the functions of the various courts had no precise definition in common law. It was possible to insult, strike, sequestrate, hold to ransom and kill one's fellows with complete impunity, and neither persons nor property were safe.

Guibert de Nogent says that "the Laon tragedies are attributable to the perversity of the bishops". He is thinking of Bishop Adalbéro Ascelin and the dramatic scenes attending the accession of the Capets, which were complicated further by a fight between burgesses and bishop, but he is thinking particularly of his contemporary, Bishop Gaudry. When it was decided to make him a bishop, Gaudry was not even in holy orders; he was a referendary of the king of England. He was a shameless, brutal creature whose sole interests in life were war and hunting. But he was thought to be rich. He was elected in 1106 amid a faint odour of simony. His pressing need for money made him burden the inhabitants of Laon with arbitrary taxes. He kept near him, to function as bodyguard and as executioner, a negro whose job was to torture, mutilate or kill anyone who resisted. If necessary, the bishop had his opponents, even the most eminent, murdered. In November 1109 he left for Rome to procure an alibi and in his absence his confederates, who included his brother and his two archdeacons, rid him of the notary of St John's Church at Laon, Gérard de Quierzy, who had slandered Gaudry and his friends. Gérard was murdered while at prayer in the cathedral, on 7 January 1110.

This was at the time when the burgesses of Noyon had just set up a commune and thus obtained certain franchises, and nothing would have been more natural than for the inhabitants of Laon to take heart from this example and rise against their oppressors. But this is not what happened. Guibert's statement is categorical. In 1111 the bishop and the local magnates, both lay and ecclesiastical, had run out of funds and were seeking means of raising money. Gaudry went off to England to ask his "friend" King Henry I for some. While he was gone, the two archdeacons and the magnates had the idea of selling the inhabitants the right to form a commune. They probably intended, once the money was in their hands, to go back on their promises, and there were probably among their number friends of Gérard de Quierzy who were glad of a chance to avenge him and to play a trick on the bishop. The burgesses accepted the offer, for which they paid a large sum, and "a conjuration of mutual aid" united by an oath "the clergy, the great men and the people".

When the bishop returned he was furiously angry and also rather worried and for a time he remained on the outskirts of the town, reluctant to enter. The sight of ready cash had a soothing effect. He swore to observe the rights of the commune as established with reference to the franchises gained by the inhabitants of Saint-Quentin and Noyon. Augustin Thierry reconstitutes these rights of the commune granted in 1111, with the help of a later charter dated 1128, but this is too precise an inference. Guibert's appraisal of the scope of the communal pact in general and subsequent events only permit the following conclusions: that the lords of the town renounced the arbitrary *taille* and gave an undertaking to demand nothing more; that the rate of fines was determined; and that the population elected magistrates. King Louis VI, for a consideration, in his turn confirmed the commune.

The oaths that had been sworn were immediately violated. An attempt was made to reintroduce serfdom. The inhabitants of Laon were prosecuted and deprived of their property. The bishop set about coining false money. After ordering one of his peasants' representatives to have his eyes put out, he had to make yet another trip to Rome to obtain a pardon. But no sooner was he back than he determined to abolish the commune. For this he needed the complicity of the king of France, so he invited him to spend the Easter festival at Laon. Louis VI arrived on

Maundy Thursday, 18 April 1112. That very day the commune was called in question, and the royal counsellors put the king's decision up for auction to the highest bidder; the inhabitants offered 400 *livres*, the bishop and great men 700. The king agreed to the abolition of the commune, but he felt uneasy and made a clandestine escape from the town the very next morning. Gaudry thought it would be an easy matter to quell the popular unrest and attempted to recoup the 700 *livres* he had given the king by levying a tax. Then, on 26 April, a savage insurrection broke out, to shouts of 'Commune! Commune!'. Forty inhabitants had sworn to kill the bishop and his accomplices.

The rebels' ringleader was a serf from the abbey of St Vincent, called Thiégaud, who was notorious for his violent nature. The bishop knew him well, in fact he had given him the nickname Ysengrin, the wolf, because he was so fearsomely ugly. Thiégaud had been employed as a tollkeeper on a bridge; it was said that he robbed travellers, throwing into the river anyone who protested. He led the attack on the bishop's residence. The bishop, after an attempt at resistance, took fright, hid in his store-room and had himself shut in a cask. Thiégaud found where he was and dragged him out of his hiding place by the hair. Then his head was split open with an axe. The nobles and clergy who escaped this massacre fled, their houses were pillaged and burned down, and the cathedral caught fire and was partially destroyed. Now the rebels were in possession they had every reason to fear the king's anger. They tried to make an ally of the notorious brigand lord, Thomas de Marle. But Thomas hesitated, and finally refused to defend Laon; he cared little for these tradesmen and wine-growers and contented himself with promising asylum on his domains to all those who wished to take refuge there. The town was abandoned; both nobles and peasants took advantage of the situation to sack the houses belonging to the burgesses from top to bottom.

The king, deeply involved in wars with his barons and with the king of England, and preoccupied also by the communal insurrection at Amiens, did nothing to check the disturbances at Laon and the surrounding area. On 6 August the abbess of St John's of Laon was murdered. However, it would seem that Bartholomew de Vir, who became bishop in 1113, succeeded in reviving the counter-revolutionary party. During Lent, in 1114, Thiégaud was arrested as he emerged from a hearty meal at which he had gorged himself and become thoroughly drunk, and was hanged. On 29 August of the same year the cathedral, now restored, was "reconciled" and consecrated. The archbishop of Rheims was present at the ceremony, surrounded by five bishops of his province. He went up into the pulpit and took as the text of his sermon a sentence from the first Epistle of St Peter: "Servants, be subject to your masters with all fear." He insisted that servants should obey their masters, not only when they were good and reasonable, but even when they were cantankerous – *sed etiam dyscolis*. The archbishop went on to say that serfs should not use the hardness and avarice of their lords as a pretext, and that communes were "detestable". This was precisely the moment when Guibert of Nogent was compiling his memoirs but he gives no hint that the archbishop's provocative homily aroused any protests. The revolutionaries had been tamed.

But Thomas de Marle was not. He had been excommunicated for offering asylum to the rebels, and now he spread terror throughout the countryside. He had wrested from the abbey of St John of Laon the two villages of Crécy and Nouvion, had fortified them and had turned them into "a dragons' ditch and a den of thieves", as Primat, the thirteenth-century French translator of Suger, puts it. Louis VI, in response to urgent requests of the prelates assembled in council at Beauvais (6 December), finally made his appearance in the Laonnois in Lent 1115, and brought Thomas de Marle to his knees. Any escaping rebels who crossed his path were hanged and their bodies left without burial. He entered Laon with ease, and stern reprisals put an end to the first communal uprising. Pope Calixtus II was able to pause for a while at Laon in 1119, and in 1124 the town raised a contingent for the army which Louis VI assembled to drive back the German invasion.

Shortly after this, however, the communal party regained the ascendant and, on 26 August 1128, Louis VI granted with the consent of and on the advice of his nobles and the citizens of Laon, an institution of peace, which was a harmless synonym for the word 'commune'. In the royal charter the mayors and *jurés* are mentioned as if they were magistrates already in office. Who were these people who, without waiting for their lords' permission, had re-established a sworn association? We do not know. There is in the charter a clause granting an amnesty to the perpetrators of past crimes, committed either before the town was destroyed, that is, before the first revolution, or before the present institution of peace. Thirteen persons are named as being excluded from the amnesty. Their names, except for one, that of a serf, tell us nothing about them at all. Augustin Thierry reproduces this list in great excitement. He tells us "I cannot help re-reading these obscure names: an ardent passion for justice and the conviction that they were superior to their state in life had torn these men from their crafts, from their trade, etc." But there is no guarantee that these thirteen men were "noble hearts"; indeed, the fact that they were abandoned to their fate by their party probably indicates that, like Thiégaud before them, they had stained their hands with crime. But their acts of violence probably helped to give the lords of the town and the king food for thought. As a result the *proceres* and the *cives* came to terms. The *proceres* conceded judicial guarantees, the total abolition of mortmain, an alleviation of the burdens of serfdom for those serfs who were allowed by their lord to be members of the commune. The charter was far from being entirely clear, and it still contained many seeds of strife. There was still trouble in store for Laon.

It may be doubted whether the *institutio pacis* of Laon reflected any serious pacific intentions. Too much innocent blood had been shed, too many people had been hanged out of hand, too much property acquired by honest toil had disappeared, for this fierce population, mainly made up of hot-tempered wine-growers, to forget such a tragic past, the memory of which was still green. For their part the lords of Laon, the nobles and clergy, remained suspicious and reserved. Elsewhere, however, I think that agreement between the two sides was often sincere, and that the synonym used in the Laon charter carried in many cases its full meaning.

The full political vocabulary of the twelfth century which was being hammered out in the seigneurial chanceries is significant. *Communia*, in the charters granting a sworn association, can be replaced by *pax*, which has exactly the same meaning. In the Montdidier charter, the scribe sometimes uses the work *pax*, sometimes *communia*. Occasionally the two words are coupled together, as in the charters of Tournai, Hesdin, and the communal village federation of Crandelain, Trucy, Courtecon, Malval, Colligis and Lierval. Or else the king or lord specifically states that permission to form a common bond is granted "for the peace of the country", "for the preservation of peace", "with a view to the future preservation of peace"! Peace! Was this not, as has been said, "the cry which arose then from every mouth"? This frequent unanimity was sometimes expressed in the charters. The lord of Labroye near Hesdin, took into account, he said, the general will, and the advice tendered by his mother, brother and sister, his nobles and the inhabitants of Labroye.

It is commonly said that the Church displayed a hatred of the communes. On the whole this is fairly true, and it could even be said that reports made to the Holy See maintained this atmosphere of dislike at the heart of the Roman curia. There is nothing surprising about this. We must not only appreciate the financial apprehensions of bishops and abbots who had vast domains to manage, made intelligent use of them, and felt the interest of the community threatened. We must also realize the state of mind of a prebendary, of a simple monk who observed the communal revolution, saw the inhabitants of the town banding together, choosing leaders, organizing their civic duties themselves, trying criminals, and infringing ecclesiastical privileges. The social order as he saw it, instituted by God to last for ever, was being overthrown. If he was a good and virtuous man he certainly cared for the needy, but he believed that nothing but charity could alleviate their lot. He did not live from hand to mouth like the unlettered masses. He had absorbed theories: the churchman must pray, must help the poor and the sick, and above all lead men into the way of salvation; the knight does battle for others, and if need be ensures order and justice by force of arms; the peasant and the tradesman work and are obliged – the reader should bear in mind the sermon preached by the archbishop of Rheims (p. 56 above) – to obey their lords even if they are evil. Anything else would lead to confusion and sin.

To arrive at a reasoned appraisal of the opinions and attitude of the Church, one should not attach undue importance to the diatribes of the chroniclers and preachers. Their ignorance of economic necessity and the conditions of progress, the poverty of their complaints, the emptiness of their thought, the insincerity of their judgement, are striking. All they are prepared to recall of the communal movement, of civic fraternity, of productive 'friendship' which so often re-established order, ensured respect for custom, restored prosperity to the city, are its sporadic excesses. It is impossible for the entire clergy to have been so blind. Even so, the preachers do tend to inveigh against society as a whole. It would be interesting to make a numerical comparison of well-known examples of fierce local struggles between Church and commune and the cases where both lent each other mutual support with fairly good grace. In walled cities like Beauvais, Amiens, Noyon, Soissons, Senlis, rules were drawn up for the maintenance of normal relations between the clergy and the commune which, despite one or two quarrels, inevitable in an age of violent passions, was in no way regarded as an element of disorder. Far from it – and this is the point I wish to make; it often happened that bishops or churches encouraged the formation of a commune on their domains because they wished to get rid of a local tyrant, or else because they thought this a reasonable price to pay for the re-establishment of order.

One of the oldest examples known to us of a communal revolution (which proved abortive) is that of Le Mans in 1069: to resist Geoffrey of

Mayenne the inhabitants of Le Mans "form a *conspiratio* they call commune and bind themselves by oaths". The bishop joined them and went with them to lay siege to the château of Sillé. It is known for certain that there was at Beauvais before the close of the eleventh century a commune on which the bishop relied to uphold his authority and, in particular, to resist his enemy the castellan. Baudry, bishop of Noyen, in the notification (1108 or 1109) which has already been mentioned, states he has "made a commune at Noyen", by agreement with the clergy, knights and burgesses. In view of the fact that, before his enthronement, the church of this walled town had, in the words of a letter written ten years previously, "suffered countless shipwrecks and been oppressed by the storms of persecutions", one may reasonably deduce that the formation of an urban sworn commune seemed to Baudry a way of ensuring peace to the greater good of his church.

The commune of Amiens owed its origin to a coalition formed against the count of the town between Bishop Geoffrey and the burgesses. "King Louis", we are told by the abbot of Saint-Riquier in 1126, "came to Saint-Riquier and established a commune between our men for our own benefit." The commune of Ham was established and sworn for the glory of God and the honour of the Church and the protection and defence of all the Church's property. At Compiègne there was in Louis VII's day a violent conflict between the secular clergy who had been dispossessed of the abbey of St Cornelius because of "enormities" they had committed, and the monks who had recently taken it over; the clergy, "relying on the power of their relatives", had driven out the monks. The king reinstated the monks in the abbey and, at the request of the abbot and in agreement with the archbishop of Rheims and the abbot of Saint-Denis, granted the burgesses a commune. All the inhabitants, within or without the ramparts, whatever developments the town might undergo, had to be "in the same oath". Clearly the king wished to bring to heel a small aristocracy of clergy and burgesses hostile to reformist ideas and, with the consent of powerful prelates, had espoused the cause of the sounder section of the clergy who were supported by the majority of the population. He declared he had acted for the sake of peace and in the interests of the Church and the safety of God's servants.

In the Laonnois itself we may observe that out of four rural federated communes, the abbey of St John at Laon had founded one and enlarged another, for it was this church which created the "peace and commune" of Crandelain, and it encouraged and enlarged the one at Cerny. In 1217, the abbess of Origny asked Philip Augustus to set up a commune between the inhabitants of Chaudardes, Cuiry, Beaurieux and Craonnelle, "to keep the peace".

It also happened that a seigneurial dynasty, or possibly the king himself, thought it useful to encourage the formation of the communal bond as a means of defence against the covetousness and brutality displayed by the petty feudal lords of the region. The commune thus became an element making for order and peace in an area where the "powerful" were attempting to maintain their habits of plunder. It was the same idea which prompted Louis the Fat to set up a commune at Mantes, the count of Eu, John I, to grant one to the poor and to the rich of his town of Eu, and the counts of Ponthieu to grant a very great number of communes. It should be added that, at least initially, the burgesses succeeded in convincing the counts of Ponthieu of the wisdom of this political precept by purchasing from them with hard cash the permission to associate by oath; which, however, was never more than verbal permission.

William Talevas, who was count of Ponthieu in 1103–1126, "sold the commune to the burgesses of Abbeville because of the abuses and vexations constantly inflicted on them by the powerful of his lands, and the burgesses received no authentic document concerning this sale". This is how Count John put it in a charter of 9 June 1184: "since it is easier to remember what is written down", and at the request of the inhabitants of Abbeville, he granted them a public instrument authenticating the granting of a commune "to be held in perpetuity *against* all comers". Similarly, Count William II, in 1202, granted the burgesses of Doullens a public instrument announcing the common bond which Count Guy II (1126–1147) had, for a consideration, allowed them to set up as a defence against the local magnates. The same formulae recur in another document of his, officially setting up the commune of Ponthoile, which Countess Ele, wife of William Talevas, had granted verbally. Again, the same reason is given by William in 1199, when granting a commune to the inhabitants of the Marquenterre region and the inhabitants of Waben.

The characteristic formula "commune to be held against all comers" recurs in the charters of Hiermont (1192), Crécy (1194), Noyelles (1195), Ergnies (1210) and Port-le-Grand (1218). At Airaines, some of the local inhabitants found it advantageous to enter into an association by oath "so that each one should help in the preservation of his neighbour as if he were his brother, if the need arose", and their example prompted the burgesses of the town to do likewise, particularly as they were encouraged by the two co-suzerains of the viscounty, Henry of Airaines and Aleaume of Fontaine; they were, in fact the first to take the oath, and they presented the inhabitants with a little charter, *cartulam*, on this occasion, which Count Simon and his wife confirmed later, in 1234.

It is clear from the opening phrases of many charters that, in the twelfth century, the essential purpose in forming a communal bond was usually to ensure safety, public order, and honest justice by promises of mutual aid. It is also clear that there was an overriding desire to have done with habits of violence and brutality, quarrels and outrages between fellow citizens, and also the threats of pillage and murder which kept away foreign traders and set townspeople and dwellers in the suburbs against each other. All this can be deduced from the communal oath itself.

The oldest surviving example of what can properly be termed the text of a communal oath from the north of France probably does not entirely correspond to the oaths taken in the eleventh or twelfth centuries. It is the oath taken by the new burgesses of Noyon in the early fourteenth century; a phrase relating to the payment of a "portion of the town's debts" is obviously quite a recent addition. But much older documents make it clear which promises were originally required. The *Établissements* of the commune of Saint-Quentin, which we examined earlier, specify in the opening lines that the burgesses, knights and clergy of the town, by permission of Count Herbert IV of Vermandois (1045–1080), swore to keep the commune saving fealty to God, St Quentin and the rights of the count and countess. They swore common aid, common counsel, common *détenance* and common defence. At Abbeville the charter of 1184 certainly did no more than repeat the wording of an oath dating from the beginning of the century, in its opening article: "It has been established and confirmed under solemn oath that each man will provide his *juré* [i.e. fellow – *juré*] with such loyalty, support, aid and counsel, as will be required by law." Here is a more precise statement made somewhat later: according to the charter granted by Louis VII to the town of Senlis in 1173, the inhabitants "swore that they would help each other as they thought right and that they would not allow anyone to steal anything from anyone or tax him or take from him anything at all belonging to him". In the charter granted by Philip of Alsace, sanctioning the laws and customs of the *amitié* of Aire in 1188, are the words: "All the members of the town's fellowship have stated by their word and oath that each will help the other as if they were his brothers in anything useful and honest."

Coming to the thirteenth century, we find that the document granting a commune to Crépy-en-Valois, in 1215, begins as follows: "We, having regard to the peace which must in future be observed, have agreed that a commune be set up in Crépy which everyone residing in Crépy and living around the castle has sworn to observe for ever. They have sworn to help each other if they think it right, and not to allow anyone to take anything from anyone or to levy a tax on him." Further on it is specifically stated: "If anyone wishes to join the commune, he must swear the communal oath." At Rue-en-Ponthieu, when a new burgess swears the commune he is told that if he should hear, either by night or day, the ringing of the bell named Moinel, he is to come bearing arms and join the mayor; if he hears someone shouting 'commune!' at an outsider he is to help his fellow *juré* like a brother, even outside the town wall.

The precise value of such promises and their actual consequences may be seen in detail by reading charters like the one granted to Péronne. Those who formed an association by means of the communal oath are pledged to help each other even by main force. If one of them is attacked by a man who does not belong to the commune, his fellows, *vicini de communia*, will give him armed support, and unless someone is killed, no punishment will be incurred for becoming involved in the dispute. If anyone withholds his help, the mayor must "cry on them the dishonour they have brought to the commune". The members of the commune are also protected against each other. If a dispute arises between two members, they must accept the arbitration imposed by the mayor. At Aire, where the commune was known as the *amitié*, a man who has insulted his "friend" must pay him five sous and pay five sous to the 'leader' of the *amitié*, the *prefectus amicitie*. The Bray-sur-Somme charter adds that outside the town it is also forbidden to prosecute one's fellow-citizen for motives of hatred *per odium prosequi*, for that would be an infringement of the commune. We must add that this peaceful association, the commune, precludes all possibility of other sworn alliances within its territory.

For example, in 1232 at Abbeville two factions had been formed, the members of which had taken an oath; the echevins of Amiens were instructed by the count of Ponthieu to try the partisans who were plunging the town into strife and bloodshed, and those who had joined together on oath without renouncing the communal oath were fined. And those who had, at one and the same time, entered into this federation by oath and abjured the commune, were severely punished: in addition to a huge fine of sixty *livres*, they suffered the penalty of having their houses pulled down.

In the course of this study of the commune regarded as an *institutio pacis* we have quoted texts from the eleventh, twelfth and early thirteenth centuries. But with the passage of time the general anarchy diminished perceptibly in France and the need for peaceful associations consequently grew less. And so a different preoccupation was now to dominate the minds of kings and great lords when they granted a commune, namely a desire to derive from it the same benefits as they had done from a vassal.

3. *Servitium regis*

From the earliest days of the communal movement, Louis VI and VII had realised, even though intermittently, that sworn associations of burgesses could further the monarch's activities. Historians of the early Capetians have made a careful study of their policy, which was incidentally somewhat uncertain and opportunist, and we need not repeat their findings. However, there are still points worthy of mention and elucidation as regards Philip Augustus' intrigues and the initiatives taken by his counsellors at the beginning of his reign. These counsellors hoped to foster the development of sworn associations in the major fiefs so as to assume the role of protectors, as is evident from a study of the history of the Dijon commune which should have been given greater prominence.

In the twelfth century the dukes of Burgundy were poor and weak. Hugh III was refused homage by the lord of Vergy whose seigneury was near Dijon; he was a vassal to be reckoned with. War broke out between them in 1183. The king intervened to compel the duke to indemnify the churches whose domains had been laid waste. It was in these circumstances that Hugh III, in an attempt to win over the inhabitants of Dijon, allowed them to form a commune and granted them the liberties enjoyed by the members of the Soissons commune. This charter has not survived, and indeed they may have contented themselves with a verbal concession. There is, however, still in existence an original diploma issued by Philip Augustus (between 1 November 1183 and 31 March 1184), which is most curious.

At the request and desire of the duke [of Burgundy] and his son, we take charge of the said commune, to preserve and maintain it, in such a way that, should the duke or his heirs attempt to infringe the said commune or to annul the institution of the commune, we shall, to the best of our ability, try to make him uphold it. If the duke is unwilling to do this for us, we shall receive the inhabitants together with their property, in our territory and provide them with a safe conduct.

Here we have an unprecedented situation: the king is threatening the duke with facilitating the exodus of the inhabitants of Dijon and receiving them in his domain. It is clear that there was, in fact, collusion between the king and the burgesses so as to establish the commune. Moreover, soon afterwards the king openly supported the lord of Vergy, who took refuge on royal territory in 1186 and submitted his lordship to the king. The duke signed a treaty of alliance with Henry, king of the Romans, and war broke out between the king of France and his vassal. The duke of Burgundy was obliged to cry mercy and pay a heavy fine. He granted the inhabitants of Dijon the 1187 charter, and Philip Augustus confirmed it: if the duke violated it, it was understood that within forty days after receiving the complaint, the king's court would determine the amount payable to the commune.

This is the most striking surviving example of the patronage exerted by Philip Augustus over a commune in a major lay fief. Not that the king expected the people of Dijon to give him any military support. These wine-growers had no stomach for going to war for the benefit of a third party. They had purchased exemption from their military service from the duke in 1185. The most the king could hope for was to use them to create trouble for the duke if the need arose. But this was by no means the general picture; we must now deal with the major innovation which characterizes the policy of Philip Augustus and his rivals the Plantagenets towards the communes.

A new concept of the services which could be rendered by the communal sworn association regarded as a collective feudal entity which could be treated like a vassal, was current in France for about half a century, approximately from 1175 to 1225. The documents which prove this are the acts of Philip Augustus and the statistics drawn up by his chancery, and on the other hand the decrees of the early Plantagenets in their capacity of lords of Normandy, the Loire provinces and Aquitaine. In Philip Augustus' reign there was indeed a genuine political alliance between the monarchy and the burgess class, and economic factors are in no way sufficient to account for the development of urban liberties at this time. At the same time the Angevin Empire was established, as a result of Henry Plantagenet's accession to the English throne, and Henry II, Richard Lion-Heart and John had the task of maintaining their rule over the greater part of France as it then was, from the Channel to the Pyrenees, and of dealing with a number of towns in mid-development which were often turbulent and demanding. But internal difficulties and wars fought with ever-increasing ferocity, which arose from the mere fact of the existence of the Angevin Empire, obliged them to make concessions to the burgesses and even to request their services. It was then that the idea occurred to them that the communal association, which was still a vigorous and often a pugnacious institution, was just as able as noble vassals to supply valuable aid, and for this reason the prudent course would be to favour the retention or the establishment of communes.

Giry, when pursuing his researches into the *Établissements* of Rouen and the related charters, whether of Normandy or Poitou, had remarked that municipal liberties of this type created between the lord and the burgesses a bond similar to that which united the suzerain and the vassal: there was the same preoccupation on the part of the lord with the search for military forces, and the essential obligations were comparable. This led Giry to represent the French commune as a feudal entity, and even to infer from this (which is inadmissible) a definition which neglected the true character of the commune. Similarly, Luchaire wrote: "The towns, raised to the dignity of communes and invested with a certain sovereignty, with the right to appoint their magistrates and to be self-governing, ceased to belong to the class of commoners or villeins. As collective lordships they became members of Feudal Society." They were "genuine popular lordships organized on military lines. A new feudal element was demanding its place in the sun".

In his book on the French communes which appeared in 1890, Luchaire adduced proofs of this doctrine of the collective popular lordship and strove to show that the communes had the obligations and rights of a vassal. Finally, in his *Manuel des institutions françaises* (1892) he included in the category of collective popular seigneuries or lordships the great consular republics of the south of France.

In 1933 an American scholar, Carl Stephenson, a pupil of Pirenne, disputed the validity of this doctrine, which had gained almost universal acceptance in France and had influenced the teaching of medieval history. In his book *Borough and town*, an important work on municipal origins in England, written to show the close link between English towns and the towns of the continent, particularly in France, he devoted an appendix entitled 'Giry and Luchaire on the commune' to a refutation which his disciples regarded as definitive. In his view, all the facts marshalled by historians to prove that the communes and the consular republics of the south of France had a feudal and seigneurial character are also found in the history of the other free towns. Stephenson's demonstration is teeming with errors, and it would be hard to understand how such an experienced scholar could have been led to make such stubborn denials, but for the glimpse of the cloven hoof in the conclusion of his book. The feudal theory of the commune is condemned, he maintains, both by its inherent weakness and because of its incompatibility with any general explanation of municipal development in Western Europe. This loyal disciple of Pirenne was unable to accept a thesis which seemed to him to attack the dogma that history is only explicable in terms of economics. The whole of municipal development in the West was conditioned by the revival of trade, geographical situation, roads, markets, and the progress of the merchant class. In Stephenson's view anything departing from these principles is mistaken. Unfortunately, principles and consequences form a vicious circle.

If we wish to confirm that the communes in Philip Augustus' time had a certain military character, we need only return to the chancery document in which we have already found the proof that they formed a separate group and that the word 'commune' had a technical sense. I refer to the list of the communes of the king of France, which figures in the oldest register belonging to Philip Augustus, an apparently incoherent jumble of large towns, small towns, villages even, to which the kings of France had granted the right to form sworn associations, and from which they expected service – *servitium regis*.

What service? *Pace* Mr Stephenson, this is first and foremost military service, that is to say, the essential feature of the feudal obligation. This register of Philip Augustus provides, as I have stated above, a list of ecclesiastical and lay vassals, which ends with the enumeration of thirty-nine communes. If this enumeration is compared with another set of contemporary statistics, the *Prisée des sergents*, it becomes clear that these communes must all, without exception, owe contingents of sergeants, whereas Paris, Orléans, Étampes, Bourges, Montargis, Gien, Lorris, etc., which are not or have ceased to be communes, pay a tax in lieu.

The feudal and military character of the communes in the reigns of Philip Augustus and Louis VIII and the regency of Blanche of Castile, is an incontrovertible historical fact. Not without good reason does the mayor appear on the seal of many communes as an effigy of a warrior fully armed, sometimes on horseback and galloping, as if he were a lord. It was, in fact, the mayor who commanded the militia. He led into battle rugged fellows bound to their military duty by the communal oath and by the threat of dire penalties. These burgess militiamen of Philip Augustus' time were not the free-archers of Bagnolet any more than the militiamen of the Flemish *villes à loi*, who 100 years later routed the cavalry of the king of France. The great consular towns in the south of France had the same warlike aspect. Carcassonne was a huge fortress. Toulouse defended itself so valiantly against Simon de Montfort that he was unable to take it. It was an aggressive lordship which, in the early thirteenth century, waged wars and concluded peace treaties with the neighbouring barons.

Carl Stephenson could not even have taken refuge in an assertion that the obligations of the burgesses in the big towns did not go beyond the general obligations of commoners and were not feudal in character. To contemporaries this was indeed a feudal service; the assimilation is clearly shown in certain texts. The charter granted by Philip Augustus to the town of Poitiers in 1222 states that: "The citizens owe us military service and riding service (*chevauchée*) beyond the Loire in all the places where our men of the fiefs of Poitou owe it to us."

The same must be said of the financial aid owed to the lord. Certainly the towns, as subject towns, were obliged to give financial help or *aide*, and Carl Stephenson is as familiar with the facts as any other historian. But he must not deny us the right to compare the *aide* supplied by a commune with the *aide* supplied by a vassal, for we have the example of the Ponthieu communes which quite clearly owed feudal *aide aux trois cas*. We read in the Abbeville charter: "The burgesses are required to pay me only three taxes: 100 *livres* of Ponthieu for my son's knighthood, 100 for my daughter's marriage, and 100 for my ransom." In the Ergnies charter, which derives from it, the *aide* in these three cases amounts to forty *livres* of Ponthieu; the figure is the same in the Airaines charter; in the Poix charter it amounts to sixty *livres*.

Once the situation arose in which the essential obligations of the noble vassal, namely the duties of military service and *aide* in the three *cas* or categories, were also present in the relations between communes and their lords, it is not surprising that the specific features of vassalage should be encountered in their historic form. There are a few surviving texts of the oath of feudal loyalty sworn by the communes. At Laon, there were disputes on this matter between the commune and the bishop, whose suzerainty the commune refused to accept. Both sides accepted the arbitration of the archbishop of Rheims. He decided that the mayor and *jurés*, and then all the inhabitants, should pronounce the following oath: "I swear to you, Lord Garnier, bishop of Laon, that I will preserve your life, your limbs and your earthly goods, in good faith, saving the fealty given to our lord the king" (11 July 1239).

In 1228 they had sworn to the king to preserve to the best of their power "his body, his limbs, his life and his earthly goods". In that same year, at Amiens, the commune repeated the same formula and added that it would adhere to the king and the queen his mother "against all men and women who may live and die". An oath sworn by the Périgueux commune in 1204 comes still nearer to feudal acts of homage, for it is there stated that the commune will surrender the town "to large or small force", each time it is required to do so by the king its lord. The king appears in these documents only as a feudal lord, and in every case the formulae are the same when the commune swears an oath of fealty to a bishop or to a count. These are the feudal formulae.

Occasionally the word 'homage' is found. At the time when the burgesses of Châteauneuf-de-Tours persisted, in spite of annulments and prohibitions, in regarding themselves as a commune, and when Philip Augustus and Richard, king of England and count of Anjou, were engaged in determining their respective rights and those of St Martin's of Tours, it was learned that the burgesses had decided that twelve of them "for them and for the others, would do homage to the count for the safeguarding of the person and property of the men of Châteauneuf, saving the fealty owed to the king and the Church". However, declaring oneself to be somebody's man was quite an everyday ceremony. Liege homage itself was not exclusively reserved for relationships between nobles: in 1204 a sergeant of the bishop of Noyon paid him liege homage for the office of lay churchwarden. The formula of homage was required of towns which were not communes, for example peasant settlements. The important thing was the promise made by the communes to provide the services typical of vassalage.

In return for these undertakings of loyalty and aid, the lord promised his protection. For example, the bishop of Laon, in 1239, immediately after the taking of the oath by the commune, declared he would preserve the persons and property of the inhabitants, together with the peace they enjoyed through the charter of their lord the king. Similarly, at Noyon, the bishop "promises to the mayor and *jurés* to preserve their rights and customs". In 1261 the young count of Artois, Robert II, on first entering the town of Saint-Omer, swore according to custom to be its "good and faithful lord" and to maintain and defend the town and the burgesses.

It is not surprising that kings, in particular Philip Augustus, should regard the burgess associations of communes, and the French barons, as comparable; this was a period when the concept of nobility had not yet become set in a narrow mould and when, despite the apparent contradiction, people thought feudally, just as in some countries at the present time, people think democratically. There is a further proof of this assertion. The judicious use which Philip Augustus made of the system of cautions is well-known. In order to procure guarantees he placed the communes and the barons on the same footing. In 1206 he sent Bartholomew de Roye to Courtrai to persuade the communes and the barons of Flanders and Hainault (because of their importance he treated the *villes de keure* as if they were *villes de commune*), to swear an oath guaranteeing the conventions agreed between the king and the count of Namur. If the count of Namur broke them, "the barons and communes and all the knights of any renown will do him harm and will help the king". In 1225, when Louis VIII restored Ponthieu to the wife of the traitor Simon of Dammartin, she was obliged to make the communes of the county swear that they would side with the king if the countess or her heirs left his service. The expression 'hereditary fief' is actually used in the same sentence as 'commune' in the little charter of the *chaussée* of Eu of about 1151: "I have granted and given this commune as a hereditary fief to the burgesses of Eu", says their count.

There is, therefore, no reason to reject the feudal theory of the commune. But, I hasten to add, it is a theory which must be stripped of its inessentials. Luchaire's teaching on the commune is hesitant and it lacks clarity. At times he indulges in word-spinning. When he speaks of "towns which have been raised to the dignity of communes, invested with a certain sovereignty and, because they are collective seigneuries have become members of feudal society", he is using fine phrases with no basis in reality. The formation of a commune was not an added dignity, and there were communes which were not invested with any sovereignty. Luchaire never adopts the jurist's standpoint, yet this is precisely the standpoint from which to define the commune and describe its evolution in the twelfth and thirteenth centuries. We have seen that in the twelfth century the lord's grant consisted in the recognition or the creation of a sworn association and was occasioned mainly by the need for peace and security within the towns. Subsequently, the kings and great barons of France, struck by the benefit they could derive from these sworn associations in the defence of their territory, positively accepted and even encouraged the formation of these communes. The feudal character of the commune is not, therefore, as a study of Luchaire's works would lead one to suppose, a primary characteristic; it is a result of the alliance which sprang up late in the day between the communes and either the king or the great baron. It cannot be presented as a constituent of the commune, or figure in any definition of it.

We must go further. Giry understood the problem when he compared the status of the commune *vis-à-vis* the king or great baron with the status of a vassal. But is it possible to maintain without reservations that the commune was a collective lordship? There is no doubt the commune did adopt some of the seigneurial prerogatives such as legislation, the exercise of justice and taxation. But it did not have them all. It was a vassal, but it may be doubted whether it had any vassals, except in extremely rare cases; and it probably did not exercise the right of confiscation, which is one of the corollaries of higher seigneurial justice. Moreover, as we have seen, it rarely exercised higher justice. It need hardly be said that the commune never had the right of coinage; this was also outside the competence of the middle and lesser nobility. No general validity should be attributed to documents such as those relating to a town like Tournai. It was possible to say that Tournai was "noble through and through"; King Charles VI put it like this, in letters dated 18 May 1389: "Since these provosts, *jurés*, echevins and *esgardeurs* were in former times and are now nobly founded in *corps*, law and commune, and have had and do have in the said town [of Tournai] and in the suburbs of the same all justice and seigneury, high, middle and low, with all the profits and revenues of this justice and of the domain of the said town and suburbs . . .." This lordship of burgesses, officially recognized as such, was, I believe, unique in northern France.

Luchaire was finally carried away, and his formula of "popular collective lordship" cannot, on mature reflection, be accepted without reservation; but the equation of 'commune' and 'vassal' suggested by Giry is accurate. We must now try to discover who originated this concept of the vassal commune burdened with heavy military duties, which was put into practice with such persistence and energy by Philip Augustus. It was obviously not the burgess class. They realized it was in their interest to accept such demands, but they would not have suggested them. Which king did suggest them? Louis VI and Louis VII fully understood that the commune could be a force of social cohesion, a guarantee of law and order, an *institutio pacis*, and indeed they rewarded one of the communes, Mantes, for having succeeded, in a dangerous area, in defending itself against the king's enemies. They did not, however, hit on the idea of using communal militia on the battlefield or during a siege on the same footing as their cavalry. We have almost no contemporary text dating from their reigns relating to military service owed to the king by the communes. It was the parochial and diocesan militia who provided them and their lieutenants with contingents of commoners. One can only cite a single event of this nature in this period, dating from the end of Louis VII's reign: in 1177 the burgesses of Soissons and Vailly helped the royal provost of Laon against Bishop Roger de Rozoy. Clearly, Louis VI and Louis VII has no notion of making systematic use of the communes against their enemies.

To discover who did create this system one must look in a different direction. An examination of the texts and dates shows that Philip Augustus merely followed the example of Henry II Plantagenet in his French fiefs. The significant charter is the one which Henry II granted to La Rochelle. This was a relatively new town, which had been assured of a population by the count of Poitiers William X and King Louis VII, who granted it franchises; before the accession of Henry II it had fallen into the hands of a Poitevin baron, Eble de Mauléon, who had encouraged the immigration of a great number of cosmopolitan adventurers "a crowd of natives and of foreigners who came by land and sea from all corners of the globe". A second parish had to be created in 1152. This Eble de Mauléon was a redoubtable figure who aimed to rule over Aunis and Saintonge and to prevent the seneschal of King Louis VII from drawing his rents in that area. But Henry Plantagenet and later his son Richard, whom he made count of Poitiers in 1169, undertook to tame the nobility of unruly Poitou, which, as Guillaume le Breton put it, was *instabilis fidei, sed valde bellica tellus* – a land weak in faith but strong in war. Eble de Mauléon was deprived of La Rochelle and his family was unable to obtain compensation until very much later, after the accession of John Lackland.

It was probably soon after Eble had been dispossessed of La Rochelle that Henry II granted a charter "to all his burgesses of La Rochelle, as a reward for their faithful service". It was an undated document, as was usual in Henry II's chancery, but the names mentioned in it enable us to place it between 1172 and 1178. Henry II, sitting in his court of law at Le Mans, in the presence of his son Richard, granted the confirmation of the franchises given by Count William and by Louis VII, while reserving the right, if he so desired, to try all major crimes himself or have them tried by his son. And he added: "I allow them in addition (*et iam*) to have a commune, *for the defence and security of their town and property*, saving the fealty and honour owed to me and the count of Poitiers my heir, and for all the time they make reasonable use of it." The scope of this concession is obvious. Henry II was afraid that La Rochelle, Poitou's seaport, might again fall into the grasp of factious barons. He wisely judged that the best course was to let the inhabitants of La Rochelle form a sworn association, capable of imposing cohesion on those families of varied, sometimes dubious origin, who had come to live in this place of refuge. The communal oath created a civic honour, comparable to feudal honour.

If such a thing were needed, we could find the precise explanation of Henry II's intention in the confirmation of the commune by Queen Eleanor of Aquitaine, in 1199: "We concede," she said, "to all the men of La Rochelle and to their heirs, a commune sworn at La Rochelle, so they can better defend and more completely preserve their own rights, saving the fealty owed to us, and we desire their free customs . . . to be inviolably observed, and, to maintain them and to defend their rights and those of our heirs, we wish them to wield and use the strength and power of their commune, when it may be necessary, against every comer, saving the fealty owed to us." Later, in 1208, John invited the burgesses of La Rochelle who could afford it to "buy a horse suited to his service" and he encouraged the mayor and commune – for by now La Rochelle had a mayor – to be responsible for the defence of the town themselves.

The *Établissements* of Rouen, however, cannot be cited in support of our argument, in that no concession of a commune is involved. It is difficult to determine the date of this document, but it is probably between 1160 and 1170. Its interest for us lies in Clauses 28 and 29, which regulate in detail the military service of the members of the commune, on the occasion when they have received marching orders from the king. Anyone attempting to avoid military service was at the mercy of the king, and the commune had his house pulled down. But we do not know when or in what circumstances this commune was set up which figures so prominently in the *Établissements*. It may have sprung up spontaneously during the anarchy following Henry I's death. A perusal of Clauses 28 and 29 leads me to think that the obligation to do military service was strengthened by Henry II; the second of these clauses (29) must in fact be the older of the two: "The mayor of Rouen, by order of the king, must summon the commune and lead it into battle; anyone remaining behind must do so by his order. If anyone remains behind without his permission the mayor must punish him if there are grounds for so doing, unless he has a reasonable excuse for staying behind." Clearly, Clause 28, which repeats Clause 29, developing it and *throwing the deserter on the king's mercy*, was added later. Until further evidence comes to light it is impossible to regard the Rouen commune as a ducal creation. Even so, we can regard the charter granted to La Rochelle by Henry II as the first one showing evidence of the desire to establish in France a commune with the intention of encouraging the burgesses to defend a position the king thought especially threatened.

From that time on, during the last twenty years of the twelfth century and the first years of the thirteenth, the idea was in the air: communes were needed at important strategic points, and wherever the kings of France and England were threatening each other, communes were established; they were also set up in places where Philip Augustus feared a Flemish or German invasion. The king of France did not disclose his motives, but contented himself with saying that he conceded the right to form a commune to his burgesses of such and such a town because of the love he bore them. But if one looks at the map and notes the dates, it becomes clear that his aim was to defend the Vexin or the approaches to Paris, and later to defend his annexation of Artois, the Tournaisis and Vermandois. He was prepared to allow the communes extensive and varied franchises, but he was also very demanding: in one region particularly threatened, the inhabitants of Tournai, on whom he could impose his will, owed him 300 well armed foot-soldiers each time they were asked to provide them; in certain cases the whole commune was obliged to rally to the king. When he conquered Poitou he required from the commune of Niort total, unconditional military service: "We or our seneschal," he said, "when we have summoned the said commune, can bring to the army and on campaign the inhabitants of the entire commune, and take them anywhere we wish."

The policy inaugurated at La Rochelle by Henry II was also followed by the counsellors of his successors, Richard Lion-Heart and John Lackland. Often their motives are obvious or frankly stated. We know from a thirteenth-century *reconnaissance* that the seneschal of Normandy, while King Richard was in captivity, enjoined the inhabitants of Evreux to organize themselves into a communal association, at a time when the king of France was expected to lay siege to the town, and we have the charters granted at the beginning of John Lackland's reign by the aged Queen Eleanor and her son. The *Établissements* of Rouen, an attenuated form of municipal liberty which was unlikely to worry the authoritarian Angevin monarchs, were granted or confirmed by them throughout Normandy and Aquitaine. With what aim in view? "We grant the commune to the inhabitants of Poitiers," said Eleanor in 1199, "so that they will be better able to defend our rights and their own and to preserve them more completely."

The same formula occurs in Eleanor's charter confirming the sworn commune of the island of Oléron. In 1202, when Philip Augustus invaded Normandy, John Lackland established communes at Fécamp, Harfleur and Montivilliers. "We desire," he declared, "you and the others of your locality to have a commune as long as you wish, and to prepare yourselves by means of arms and all things needful to defend our land." There is no doubt at all that John was here constituting a kind of revocable collective military fief, just as at this same period he distributed money fiefs to Flemish knights to ensure their help in war. We know from a document of his successor, at least as regards Oléron, that these concessions involved a sharp fall in revenue for the Plantagenets; they were obviously granting at the same time certain financial privileges to the burgesses. Their aim was to ensure, even at the cost of considerable sacrifices, the safety of strategic points.

Was this policy effective? Most certainly it was. This has been disputed, in view of the way the militia of Corbie, Amiens, Beauvais, Compiègne and Arras, involved in the battle of Bouvines, were in fact repulsed. But this argument has little weight; a defeat does not always prove military inefficiency. The burgesses, who arrived late on the battle-field, were worn out by the forced march they had been obliged to make, and Philip Augustus acknowledged the valour and fidelity of his communes by entrusting prisoners to their care. During his entire reign he showed his confidence in them. He recalled that at the time of his cruellest trials, in 1188, the valour of the burgesses of Mantes had saved Paris. Later, the young Louis IX was to call on the services of nineteen communes to go and punish Beauvais in revolt.

Similarly, Richard Lion-Heart and John Lackland were faithfully served by most of the communes in their French fiefs. Those which were vanquished by Philip Augustus were defeated with ease only because of John's cowardice. They deserted their lord because their lord deserted them. In this they respected the code of feudal honour.

BOOK II   THE CLOSE OF THE MIDDLE
          AGES. CRISES.
          DISAPPEARANCES. REVIVALS

CHAPTER 1

Changes in the thirteenth century

It has been said that the French communes were very short-lived. Such clichés have their place in elementary textbooks, but they can only be regarded as half-truths requiring further elucidation and must be treated with cautious reservations. It is not true that the life of the various communes was of roughly equal length; some disappeared almost at once; others lasted so long that when they finally expired the fact went unnoticed because they had long since ceased to be regarded as a commune except in certain official documents.

Nor must we fail to recognize, as has sometimes happened, the great variety of causes for the decline of the communes. Class strife, inefficient finances, a taste for domination on the part of the officials of the king or of princes, were not the only reasons, and in many cases were not even contributory factors. I have already shown that the hostility of the Church must not be presented as a constant feature.

Even when restricted, as it should be, to the geographical area in which certain *villes libres* or free towns developed from a sworn association, the history of the French communes is and remains right to the end extremely complex. I hope the reader will bear with me if I do not oversimplify it.

1. Early disappearances

We must not define the time-span of the French communes by assuming that they existed in the twelfth and thirteenth centuries and died out in the fourteenth. The truth of this assertion becomes clear if we draw up a list of communes which disappeared earlier than this, during the thirteenth or even the twelfth century: there were communes which came to nothing, or were suppressed or simply expired for reasons still not clear to us, and there were also communes which revived. On the other hand, for this early period the customary explanations will not do, because in the twelfth century the growing plutocracy had not yet become a crushing burden on the weak, financial causes had scarcely begun to operate, and the monarchy did not yet have a policy of centralization. In order to understand this more clearly we must examine specific instances.

The Le Mans commune, possibly the oldest of all the French communes, was short-lived. The same thing happened to many Norman towns which had been governed for some years by the *Établissements* of Rouen. No texts survive which offer any explanation of these cases. Probably a feeling of indifference was the reason for the disappearance of so many communes in Normandy. It was often in response to an imperious request from the king of England that the burgesses formed a sworn association when they would, in fact, have been satisfied with franchises. Elsewhere it was the hostility of the clergy – which must not be exaggerated as I have shown, but which must not be denied – which in the twelfth century nipped in the bud certain attempts at association directed against an abbatial authority. The chronicles of St Médard's at Soissons tell us that in the days of King Louis the Young and of Enguerrand, who was enthroned as abbot in 1148, a commune was set up in the village of Berny-Rivière, a dependency of the abbey of St Médard, and that it was "annulled".

These setbacks were frequent in Louis VII's reign and at the beginning of Philip Augustus' reign because the pious Louis VII did not readily disobey the reproofs of the pope and clergy, and the young Philip Augustus had not in the early years of his reign decided on his policy of alliance with the communes. The commune of Vézelay had been constituted in 1152 with the help of the count of Nevers, who hoped to wrest the overlordship of the town from the abbot, but in 1155 the abbot obtained the intervention of Louis VII with the pope's support and forced the burgesses to obey him. Another count of Nevers also encouraged the association of the burgesses of Auxerre and once again the king yielded to the requests of the ecclesiastical overlord (1175). The bishop of Châlons-sur-Marne was able to thank Louis VII for "dispersing" the "burgess fraternity" of the town, and thanks to this same king the inhabitants of Tournus had to give up the idea of forming a commune without the abbot's permission. It was at the request of the abbot of Saint-Pierre-le-Vif and on the pope's orders, *jubente Eugenio papa*, that Louis VII abolished for a time the commune of Sens, in 1147, a year after granting it. Immediately upon his succession in 1137 he had punished those responsible for a communal uprising at Orléans and dissolved the newly-formed Poitiers commune. This last show of authority was quite justified because the inhabitants of Poitiers intended to found a confederation of the towns in the county. Philip Augustus quashed the communes of Étampes and Châteauneuf-de-Tours. At Étampes it was not only the clergy who felt their privileges attacked, but also the lesser nobility.

Louis VII and then Philip Augustus even consented to the suppression of the commune of the Laonnois, after having encouraged its formation and revival. Thanks to some chroniclers' references (and they are very scanty as regards the communes), it is possible to discover more or less what happened in the Laonnois, and the facts are well worth recalling. It is a striking instance of the grinding poverty to which the serfs were reduced when the master, even though a prelate, insisted implacably on his rights. The Laonnois area to the south-west of Laon included seventeen villages, fourteen of which were dependent on the bishop and three on the chapter. The peasants were even more incensed at the servile burdens weighing on them, particularly that of *formariage*, because they could see close at hand the federal commune of Bruyères enjoying the advantages of liberty.

In 1174 the domains of the bishopric of Laon had reverted to the king after the bishop's death, and the inhabitants of the fourteen villages grouped around the most important one, Anizy-le-Château, obtained from the king, who was then provisional owner of the episcopal domains, a commune charter modelled on that of Laon. But the following year a nobleman ascended the episcopal throne, a man fonder of hunting and going to war than of performing his priestly functions; this was Roger of Rozoy, a relative of the powerful count of Hainault. He mounted an expedition to bring the inhabitants of the Laonnois to their senses, enlisting the help of his brother the lord of Rozoy, the counts of Rethel and Roucy, and the castellan of Pierrepont. On hearing this news the peasants sought help from the king, who summoned to their aid members of the communes of Laon and Soissons and the men of the abbey of St Médard at Soissons; they also had on their side some other communal militia such as the militia of Crépy and Vailly. But when, in March 1177, they were confronted, near the mill at Comporté on the River Ailette, with knights who were well armed and accustomed to warfare, they dispersed; some were killed or drowned in the Ailette and the rest were taken prisoner. Louis VII put on a show of anger and seized the bishop's temporalia or worldly goods. But he could not quarrel with the count of Hainault, who was the ally of the king of England. He gave in to his threats and the commune was suppressed in 1179, the year in which the young Philip Augustus married the count of Hainault's daughter.

The peasants of the Laonnois were sacrificed to political scheming. The episcopal yoke was so heavy that when Philip Augustus became king he took steps to lighten it. The bishop, Roger, and the delegates of the peasants, appeared before him in 1185; certain rents were fixed; the king appointed twelve echevins to try any disputes which might arise between bishops and peasants. Some years later, after a war in which the bishop had sided against the king, Philip Augustus actually approved, or so it seems, the reconstitution of the commune. But at the beginning of his crusade in the Holy Land when he was harassed by the clergy, he quashed it once and for all "wishing to avoid imperilling his soul" (Messina, winter of 1190–1191).

But the peasants were very persistent; on two occasions in the thirteenth century they made preparations for a mass emigration, but custom did not allow this. Only the most important of the villages within the federation, Anizy, obtained a charter granting franchises, and doing away with mortmain and the *formariage*. But the collective commune, which the peasants had once more tried to put together, was never mentioned again.

Members of a commune deprived of their right to associate did occasionally win the day. As we have seen, the inhabitants of the town of Laon itself, who were feared by the bishop, had their commune restored as early as 1128. Eleanor of Aquitaine reinstituted the Poitiers commune in 1199. Sens was granted a commune again by 1186 at the latest, and one wonders whether the quashing of the Étampes commune was final: when Louis VIII confirmed the freedom of the inhabitants from the lordship of Sainte-Croix d'Étampes the dean of the church of Sainte-Croix at Orléans specified that no freeman residing on his land could join the *commune* of Étampes. Perhaps the writer forgot to add: '. . . if one is ever formed again.'

In the twelfth century at Châtillon-sur-Seine and particularly at Saint-Valéry-sur-Somme, we can sense with startling clarity not only the enmity between clergy and burgesses, but also the hesitation of certain lay lords, harried by ecclesiastical complaints and obliged to sacrifice a commune against their will. At Châtillon-sur-Seine the duke of Burgundy had established a commune in 1208. The bishop of Langres, who was lord of part of the town, resisted the move, and after a protracted dispute the duke gave way. In 1233 he revoked the commune, *sive juste sive injuste posita*. At Saint-Valéry, the town had sprung up gradually around a Merovingian abbey and had been granted a commune, the date and terms of which have not come down to us. The burgesses lived on bad terms with the monks and were twice excommunicated. Finally, in the first months of 1232, they laid siege to the monks in their monastery, then in the presbytery where they took refuge, and attempted to starve them to death: they set fire to the church doors and parodied the religious ceremonies.

Pope Gregory IX, in letters addressed to Robert of Dreux, the lord of Saint-Valéry, demanded exemplary punishment and compensation. It looks very much as though Robert of Dreux, a Capetian prince and cousin to the king, was most reluctant to yield to the Church's pressure. He took two years to reach a decision. Then, after holding a council attended by the archdeacons of Rouen and Amiens and the dean of Amiens, and obviously under heavy pressure, he gave his decision, not without having "diligently examined the circumstances, and the consequences which might flow from this". His judgement kept the future open: "There will never be a bell, a belfry, a mayor, echevins, *jurés* or community in the said town and suburb, unless by the permission and consent of the monks." If he or his heirs, having obtained their consent, should re-establish the commune, two good and faithful *prud'hommes* were to be brought before the abbot and the monks each year, and they were to choose one of the two for the office of mayor; and the mayor was to swear to uphold the privileges of the abbey. The burgesses were probably not very anxious for the abbot to meddle in their affairs and preferred to do without a commune. For a century and a half there is no mention of one in the texts. Not until much later was the commune of Saint-Valéry re-established, as we shall see, and then it was without the monks' consent.

The facts I have just related attest to the difficulties attending the existence of the communes and show what energy, sometimes ill-rewarded, the burgesses had to display in order to retain their charter, even in the century when the commune was in its prime. They also prove that *communiers* were not everywhere completely convinced that their best interest lay in the sworn association. We shall encounter these causes of weakness again. The decline of certain communes, at the end of the Middle Ages, is explicable only by the extremely precarious foundations and by the indifference of those living in the building but taking no trouble to strengthen the fabric.

2. The number of communes increases. The movement comes to a halt

The early part of the thirteenth century is probably the period when the communes were most numerous in France. Outside the Capetian domain it was thought advantageous to create them, either by lords of second or third rank, for instance in Artois, or by powerful princes in Champagne or Guyenne. There were small towns whose inhabitants, harassed by the lord's agents, still saw in the sworn association the safest way of guaranteeing their rights, and the lords had good reason to dread the formation of revolutionary communes in their domains. This was the case at Maisnières, Saint-Junien and even Châteauneuf-de-Tours, which despite harsh repression in 1212 made several attempts to obtain freedom. In the royal domain and the Capetian sphere of influence it is possible to trace, at least up to 1224, the creation of fresh communes (Cappy in 1207, Bray-sur-Somme in 1210, Athis in 1212 and Beaumont-sur-Oise in 1223–1224).

On the other hand the official documents of St Louis' day, the decrees of the Paris Parlement, the theories formulated by Beaumanoir, reveal obvious respect for the privileges of the communes. There is no sign that the institution was disintegrating. Yet, despite this apparent vitality, there was, in the first third of the thirteenth century, a partial collapse of the communal institution; it was such a resounding crash that most historians make this the point at which they conclude their chapters on the French communes. But this was no sudden phenomenon, nor can external circumstances be invoked; the Hundred Years War had not yet begun. What had happened during the period which followed the last communes to be created in the royal domain by Philip Augustus and Louis VIII?

All things considered, and bearing in mind that there were sudden leaps forward, it may be said that during this period the communal movement ceased over nearly all the area we are concerned with: the mainspring had run down, the hand ceased to move.

If one examines the royal domain and the lands conquered by Philip Augustus it is possible to determine within a year or two the date when this movement lost impetus; this is a most interesting date because it reveals a close connection between the development of the communes and the needs of the monarchy since Philip Augustus ascended the throne. The decade preceding the victory of Bouvines was the period in which the granting of communes reached its peak. From that point the decline was rapid. Philip Augustus in the last years of his life, and later his son Louis

VIII, preserved friendly relations with the existing communes, but after his triumph in 1215 Philip granted little else than confirmations of communes (Ponthieu in 1221–1222, Poitiers in 1222). Louis VIII, during his brief reign, confirmed a fairly large number of communes, but established only a single new one, at Beaumont-sur-Oise.

It is by no means certain that Louis VIII was the last king to create a commune in the thirteenth century. St Louis may have granted a commune at Asnières-sur-Oise, because it appears in 1260 as one of the *villae communiarum*. This little town was unusual in that it had received from Louis VIII in 1223–24 a charter copied from that of the neighbouring commune of Chambly but was not called *commune* by the king. I shall attempt later to explain such anomalies as this. One wonders whether St Louis completed Louis VIII's charter by acknowledging explicitly that the inhabitants enjoyed the juridical privilege of *corps et collège*. We do not know.

Another obscure case is that of Aigues-Mortes – and here I am stepping outside the geographical limits I set myself. The magistrates of Aigues-Mortes were, of course, known as consuls, and the clauses in the charter regarding civil law were taken from the law current in the south of France. But in view of the motives which prompted the granting of political franchises, a comparison with the towns in the north of France would seem justified. It was important in 1246, on the eve of the crusade, to establish on the Mediterranean, in an uninhabited area made treacherous by a constant silting-up process, a royal port inhabited by loyal, energetic men. It would be a jumping-off base for the crusaders, and a place where pilgrims and traders could pause on their travels. These considerations were just as pressing as the reasons which prompted Philip Augustus to grant communes along the Anglo-Norman frontiers. The commune structure which had, half a century before, seemed the one best suited to create a spirit of initiative and self-defence, seemed the obvious choice, particularly since the inhabitants in such a remote area of France would be difficult to control. St Louis gave them considerable liberties. They were to choose each year not more than four consuls, and have a council of elected *jurés*. The king's court was to have no hand in the election. The consuls were to own a house in common in which they would meet whenever they wished, and a chest in which to store their archives. But the word *communia* was not used, and there is no trace of any collective oath binding the inhabitants together; no mention was made of the privilege of *corps et collège* nor of a bell, the supreme symbol of the commune. The word *communitas* was used only to describe the population as a whole. In view of these facts, it would be better not to classify Aigues-Mortes as a commune. Let us merely regard its history as a proof of the influence exerted by the communal movement on urban liberties and as evidence of new concepts which did not regard the obligation of fraternal aid between citizens as essential. In any event it was the beginning of St Louis' reign which marked the end of the communal movement in the specific commune area – 'France', Picardy and Normandy.

But it is not merely in this respect that I see the reign of St Louis as a turning point in the history of the communes. One of the outstanding features of this history, as seen from the standpoint adopted in this book, is the notion which enabled contemporaries to define the commune. It is a fact which has not been sufficiently stressed that, for contemporaries, the French commune changed character during the period we have now arrived at. It trod narrower, more official paths – in a word, it became part of the French legal system. I cannot stress too much the fact that it became a legal concept at the very moment when no new communes were being granted, and when the only charters issued were confirmatory.

The communes are usually presented as having immediately acquired their definitive features, which can then quite properly be described in a single chapter with paragraphs arranged in a logical sequence. The changes which took place during the twelfth and thirteenth centuries are so obvious that some historians, particularly anxious to stick closely to the facts, have noted these changes and looked for chronological divisions. Achille Luchaire, at the end of his book on the French communes, provided such a classification. He suggested that three periods be differentiated: first, one of *semi-hostility* on the part of the king; secondly, one of *alliance* between the royalty and the communes; and thirdly (in the reign of St Louis, Philip the Bold, Philip the Fair and his three sons), a period of *subjection and exploitation*. This concluding chapter of his book, called 'The three periods', would fit better in a history of the power of the monarchy. Reflections on their relations with the monarchy are certainly not out of place at the end of a book about the communes: but even assuming that these considerations are accurate, they are not enough in themselves to exhaust the question. We shall see, in any case, that they have been reduced to views which are debatable and far too summary.

The main facts, it seems to me, are these: the commune, which resulted from economic and social factors, developed spontaneously as a sworn association, then it acquired, by the strength of civic union, such vigour that kings realized it was a force they could make use of and for a time sought alliance with it; in a second period the commune suddenly lost momentum, became crystallized, became a subject for theorizing and, even in the eyes of its own members, was henceforward a privileged entity instead of being the living testimony to energetic burgess solidarity.

This second phase was naturally and causally linked with the extremely rapid progress of the monarchy and the parallel advances in legal knowledge. The officials of the royal court and of the major seigneurial law courts, and the *baillis* or bailiffs whom the royal court sent out to administer its affairs at a distance, were almost all jurists. They argued about custom. They were no longer ignorant of Roman law. The day of the legal specialist had arrived.

These men refused to accept that an association of burgesses could lay claim to any degree of independence unless its liberties were clearly defined and granted by the lord beyond a shadow of a doubt. This led them to enquire into the essential nature of the commune. They knew that ancient Rome had acknowledged the existence of legal personalities, collectivities which had obtained from the senate or the emperor an existence of their own distinct from that of the individuals composing it; they attributed to the commune this legal personality defined by the expression *jus communitatis et collegii*. The relative novelty of their views must be recognized, even though it could be challenged by the production of a number of texts from the preceding period.

There is no doubt that the communes in the twelfth century and the early thirteenth century already functioned as 'legal persons'; there was the expression 'body of the commune'; the *communia* owned property and land, *potestates*, it bought, built, leased and rented; it instituted lawsuits and had suits brought against it; it made declarations, swore oaths; the Church regarded it as a Christian personality and occasionally excommunicated it. But at that period the view was certainly not held that such things made a commune any different from another human group. The concept of legal personality was widespread. Moral persons were formed with no legal authorization and sprang up at the slightest pretext. Not only were there ecclesiastical establishments, or institutions dependent on the Church, like hospices and leper hospitals or corporations, gilds and confraternities, but sometimes a whole town or some part of it assumed a collective personality. For example, in 1150 a case was brought before King Louis VII's court at Chartres between Raoul Mauvoisin and 'the poor of the town'. In short, during the most important period of grants of commune the legal personality was not clearly defined, nor was it a privilege. In the second half of the thirteenth century it was regarded as a privilege.

The doctrine must have been elaborated at the *curia regis* in St Louis' reign, because right from the start of his successor's reign the pleas and decrees of the Paris Parlement show that it was applied as a matter of course. In two court cases brought in 1273 we read that at Pont-de-Roont *non est communia, collegium, vel aliquid tale,* and at Lyons there was *nec communia, nec universitas, nec aliquod collegium* and consequently the town could not have a seal. Ten years later, Beaumanoir in his *Livre des coutumes et des usages de Beauvaisis,* clearly differentiates by a legal criterion between 'the communities by reason of commune' and the other towns. In his chapter on *Procureurs* which must be compared with the chapter on *Compagnies,* meaning Societies, the commune is seen as a privileged society, which has the right to be judicially represented by its mayor and its *jurés,* in contrast to the *villes batèïces,* towns with no commune in which the *procureurs,* when a lawsuit is brought, are chosen by the *seigneur justicier* by agreement with the inhabitants. Beaumanoir endeavours moreover to establish that "each person in the commune severally" has wider legal powers than the community concerning the acquisition of property by purchase or by inheritance. The commune is most certainly a legal personality in the modern meaning of the word, with its legal powers and legal limitations.

How was the existence of a commune demonstrated in the eyes of the thirteenth-century legists of the king's court? It is interesting to note that no mention is made of the oath of mutual aid, which was originally the essential feature of the commune. The most important thing now is the charter whereby the lord has granted the commune along with a certain number of franchises. These franchises still included the setting up of a municipal body exercising more or less wide jurisdiction, and by this date, it would appear, it was out of the question for the commune to exist without a mayor. If the inhabitants had no charter, if they had in former times obtained no more than verbal permission to form a sworn association, it was useless for them to invoke tradition; their claim that they possessed a commune carried no weight at all. A case in point is that of the inhabitants of Chelles, who in 1318 were deprived by the Paris Parlement of "their status of mayor and commune, because they had no charter". The lawyers of the Paris Parlement took no account of the actual documents of the royal chancery which acknowledged the existence of this commune. Moreover, the commune must now have a seal, the privilege of legal personality and barons; the seal was denied on principle to *bonnes villes* such as Rheims or Lyons, which had no commune. Similarly, the chest or *arche* containing the charters of the town, and the bell to summon or warn the inhabitants, were regarded by the jurists as the attributes of the commune. This attitude is reflected in the terms of the annulment of a commune inflicted in 1295–6 by King Philip the Fair on the town of Laon, after a bloody uprising and the violation of the right of sanctuary.

> After due inquiry ... we have found the aforesaid citizens, the mayor, the *jurés* and echevins and the other governors (*rectores*) of the walled town of Laon guilty of the aforesaid offences; for which reason, ... by sentence of our court, we strip them of all rights of community and college ... and we deprive them of their charters, privileges, all legal institutions, jurisdiction, *échevinage* and office of *jurés* ... the bell, the seal the common chest ... and other objects appertaining to the corps or community ... completely and permanently, reserving the right to administer signal punishment to the members of the said community according to their faults and misdemeanours and to punish the community itself with a fine to be determined by sentence of our court.

A legal personality, separate from the component parts, endowed with judicial prerogatives and with a municipal body, and provided with material attributes which give it a distinctive character – this is how the *communitas seu pax* of Laon appears in this sentence. The word 'commune' was not mentioned (though it was subsquently, in the decree re-establishing it), or if it was, this was only in a sentence relating the fact that the rioters shouted 'Commune!'. There was no mention at all of the legitimate communal oath. It would even appear that the court regarded any association between the inhabitants of a town as felonious; it is stated in the preamble that the magistrates of the city fomented the uprising, "for which reason there is no doubt that they did not and do not avoid the suspicion of belonging to a secret society". This text speaks volumes on the state of mind of the court with regard to the communal oath, despite its regular, traditional character; the mistrust felt by the *gens du roi* for "conjurations" extended also to the oath. The conjuration was well on the way to becoming a conspiracy. This was most probably one of the reasons why an attempt was being made to define the commune by means of new characteristics which would exclude what had originally been its essential feature, namely the oath of mutual aid.

This fresh approach stands out still more clearly by contrast, if one compares the 1296 text with the act of Philip Augustus quashing the commune of Étampes a century before (1199–1200). The inhabitants of Étampes had committed the same crimes as those of Laon, namely cruel treatment of the clergy and nobility of the town. The king merely stated: "We have quashed the commune and have promised the churchmen and the knights that there will never again be a commune in Étampes." He used none of the formulae used in 1296 by the Paris Parlement, nor did he mention the right to have a community and college, or material emblems.

Nor did Philip Augustus make any reference to municipal offices, but merely stated that he was restoring to the churches and the knights of Étampes "the rights they had enjoyed before the commune". Clearly, the only thing involved was the freedom granted to the burgesses to form a sworn association. And indeed, as has been shown above, it was perfectly possible in the twelfth century for the commune to involve no genuine municipal government, but to be entrusted to a *prévôt* who collected the seigneurial revenues and administered justice. It is clear that, by contrast, one of the distinguishing marks of most thirteenth-century communes, as well as their civil personality, was that they had a mayor instead of a *prévôt* or *bailli*, and possessed the municipal offices referred to in the sentence of 1296. Indeed, the civil personality and the officers representing the commune both of which were necessary to bring an action, were two interconnected privileges.

The legal importance of the mayor and municipal officers in the thirteenth century explains, in my view, certain anomalies which have not been fully understood, in the history of some of the communes on the domain of the counts of Champagne. One of the best chroniclers of Champagne, Aubry de Troisfontaines, wrote that in 1231 "the count of Champagne created communes of burgesses and peasants in whom he placed more trust than in his knights". Thibaud IV did indeed grant, not in 1231 but in September 1230, charters of liberties to Troyes and Provins, and probably also to Bar-sur-Aube. It was at this period that the enemies of Blanche of Castile and Thibaud IV, supported or covertly encouraged by some of the Champagne barons, invaded and laid waste the count's lands but were obliged by the defection of Philip Hurepel, Louis IX's uncle, to make peace on 25 September 1230. The charters of September 1230 were obviously granted to strengthen, organize and reward the loyal service of the burgesses. The chronicler Aubry, and later Elizabeth Chapin in her book on the *Villes de foire de Champagne*, regard these as concessions of commune. Thibaud himself tends to support this theory: in the charter he granted in 1252 to the burgesses of Provins, he mentions "the other letter we gave them when their commune was formed", and his son Thibaud V, in a document dated 1268 for the same town, refers to the *abonnement* established "at the time when the commune was first granted, by our dear father, King Thibaud".

But a second perusal of the charters of 1230 for Troyes and Provins (which are almost identical) reveals that they contain no mention anywhere of a commune concession. The commune is referred to as an institution already in being. This should cause no surprise to anyone who has closely examined the documents which have come down to us concerning the earlier history of Troyes and Provins. These two towns, so rich and populous, already, despite any assertions to the contrary, possessed communes in the second half of the twelfth century. We possess an irrefutable document in the case of Troyes, an act of the archbishop of Sens dated 1190, stating that the *communia Trecensis* had caused the abbey of Saint-Loup damage estimated at 150 *livres*; a sentence had been passed against the commune, *lata contra communiam.*

The decree of 1153 in which the count of Champagne Henry I states that the men of "his commune of Provins" were exempt from some dues paid by the other inhabitants of the town, also leaves us in no doubt: a certain number of burgesses in Provins were at that time united by the communal bond. If one refers back to the true definition of the commune in the twelfth century and if one bears in mind that there were at that time communes without charters or municipal bodies, the whole thing becomes clear. In 1230 Thibaud IV, without needing to grant a commune, since it already existed, gave to Troyes and Provins a mayor and elected representatives; later at a time when, according to the code of jurisprudence created by the Paris Parlement, a charter and municipal body were most certainly necessary for a commune to exist, Thibaud IV himself declared that he had created these communes, and Thibaud V also credited him with their foundation. The only way to reconcile all these apparently contradictory texts is to admit the possibility that there was a profound change in the concept of the commune.

This change came about because of a misunderstanding of the past, because people no longer clearly remembered, or no longer wished to remember, the original nature of the commune. The institutions of municipal government assumed primary importance; I am tempted to think that the obligation to swear the ancient oath of mutual aid was often neglected: the *conjuratio* of burgesses for their own safety might well seem old-fashioned to later generations. The concept of the commune for the very reasons I have just given came nearer to that of the *ville franche*. One might also add that the concept of the *ville franche* is not static either, and that it moved closer to that of the commune. When the little town of Asnières-sur-Oise received from Louis VIII a charter of franchises, it was modelled on the commune charter of Chambly, including the oath of mutual aid between "all the men of this franchise" and the oath promising to defend and guard the honour and the rights of the king.

It is the thirteenth century which lends support to the modern theory which refuses to differentiate between a commune and a *ville franche* enjoying considerable autonomy. It is certain that, around 1224–1230, at the beginning of the reigns of Louis VIII and Thibaud of Champagne, the concept of the commune became very blurred. A *ville de franchises* like Beaumont-sur-Oise became a commune because it acquired the right to elect a mayor who assumed the powers formerly held by the *bailli* and the *prévôt*, although many of the *villes de franchises* at that time possessed a mayor. Before the concept of a commune could once more become clear-cut, fresh legal categories and the legal criterion of the moral personality had to be elaborated. But it is obvious that the concept lost a great part of its force now that it rested on a legal idea and no longer on the solidarity of living people.

The underlying cause of this altered approach was the increased confidence which the king placed in the burgess class. The communal system seemed too cramped. There was no longer any reason to rely solely on a monopoly of loyalty or reserves of devotion. Most of the towns owned by the king or subject to his control merited his reliance on them for support. And so the idea of *bonne ville* was born. The word already occurs in the time of St Louis. Later, when Philip the Fair summoned assemblies of Estates, he did not call on communes expecially, which is obviously a sign of their relative decline. He needed much wider support. He called upon all the *loca insignia* of his kingdom. When he summoned an assembly at Tours to deal with the affair of the Knights Templar in 1308, he enjoined his officers to cause delegates to be elected by "all the communes and all the towns where there is a fair or a market". Picot published these texts: 558 towns elected proctors. When, during the winter of 1318–19, Philip the Tall summoned two great assemblies of delegates from the towns for the purpose of raising money, he made no distinction between the communes and the other towns. He addressed himself to the *ville majores*; the decision they arrived at would be binding on all the town.

And so social and economic progress, which in its early days had given rise to the first sworn associations of burgesses, and also the progress of the monarchy, which for half a century had worked in close collaboration with the communes, now stood in the way of their development and even their preservation. They were also undermined from within by a malady which has not really been accurately enough defined.

Historians have discussed the internal dissension and the mutual hatred of the common people and the capitalist oligarchy which sprang up rapidly within two or three generations; they have described the disputes over the choice of mayor and *jurés*, and the veritable wars between families which were by no means confined to the nobility. This is perfectly justified, but it must be stated at the outset that these disturbances were not specific to the commune and that other kinds of town were also affected. Historians have based themselves on Beaumanoir's famous Chapter Fifty. Let us examine it afresh: "We have seen," he writes, "many disputes in the *bonnes villes*, one group against the other, for example the poor against the rich, or even the rich against each other." He is referring to *bonnes villes* in general, namely all towns of any importance by reason of the number of their population or their economic or political situation and which had to be watched over by their lord. He begins his chapter with this sentence: "The *bonnes villes* with a commune and even those where there is no commune, and where the people need to be protected . . .", and in fact this running sore of social hatred and vendettas was not caused by the communal structure; on the contrary, sworn associations in which rich and poor swore an oath of mutual aid were, *a priori*, better guaranteed against such troubles.

But it does seem to have been the communes especially which suffered from bad finances, debts and exploitation by the lord. They did not have at their head royal officers, *prévôts* or *baillis*, who in the thirteenth century constituted a select body, recruited and controlled by the *curia regis*: such officials would probably have protected them against the exactions of the great lords and the king himself (the example of the taxes which crushed the commune of Noyon is well known). They were at the mercy of a selfish or incompetent oligarchy, which abused the financial autonomy granted to many communes. Beaumanoir applies particularly to commune towns his remarks about the "rich who govern the needs of the town" and impose heavy taxes "on the community of the poor"; the latter could not see "the proper way to pursue their rights other than by attacking the oppressor". The only remedy seemed to be riot and murder.

The development of these burgess oligarchies which, as early as the thirteenth or even the twelfth century, monopolized municipal office, is one of the most striking features of the social history of this period and it has received scant attention from historians. Between the wars, French historians began to emulate the example of their German colleagues and to collect information on urban population as such, and on the growth of the great families. Espinas led the way by tracing the career of the Douai draper Jean Boinebroke, who finally succeeded in owning whole districts of the town. Then Lestocquoy discovered that as early as the twelfth century in Arras, one of the largest towns in northern France (20,000 inhabitants), the power of the echevins was a prey to men of wealth, both merchants and bankers, who can bear comparison with the great Italian financiers of the thirteenth century. They lent enormous sums at high interest rates to the princes and the towns of the area, and they led a life of splendour. They had inaugurated a regime of misappropriation of funds, abuse of power and acts of violence which met with little resistance: they were universally feared.

At Dijon, at an early date, wealthy family groupings were formed in the Bourg Saint-Bénigne; with the support of the knights of the *castrum* they gained control of the *échevinage*, with the result that as early as 1235 the duke tried to react and to forestall this monopoly. Even in the towns without any major trade or industry there grew up in the thirteenth century a plutocracy which thrived on speculation, on profitable tax farms and unlawful awards of contract, and lastly on the exploitation of agricultural property. These dabblers in big business were hard on the poorer folk when it suited them to be elected mayor.

In places where the development of an egoistical capitalism was neither swift nor complete, the moral and technical level of the *échevinages* sank, for a different reason. At the very time when the court and the royal and seigneurial offices were being filled by educated and capable men, the communes began to lack good "rectors", to use the expression occurring in the decree of 1296. These two phenomena were interrelated. The royal and seigneurial offices attracted young, educated, intelligent burgesses and so the urban personnel could not be kept up to strength, and consequently they diminished and disintegrated. Edouard Maugis has shown very clearly that a multiplicity of royal offices which were lucrative and were held for life, offering unlimited future prospects, discouraged the elite of the French bourgeoisie from soliciting elective offices which, being renewed annually, were unstable and limited. The result was that urban administration lost its members to monarchical and seigneurial administration. Its ranks were then filled with mediocrities out for their own advantage.

It was so difficult to find a good mayor that attempts were made in the north of France to call on people from outside the town, so we are told by the author of the *Book of justice and pleas* (probably Beaumanoir's father). When discussing municipal elections, he does in fact tell us that the burgesses of a town, instead of electing a mayor from amongst their own number, could present a request to the king to allow them to have some specific outsider as their mayor. For example, the mayor of Crépy-en-Valois, who had discharged his functions to the advantage of the inhabitants, was asked for by the burgesses of Compiègne. Similarly, the burgesses of Senlis wished to entrust the conduct of their affairs to a mayor who had shown his ability at Pontoise; the burgesses of La Rochelle, Rouen, Sens and Hesdin also attempted to use the same procedure to obtain a better administration.

It was known to historians that Bayonne had had recourse to outsiders to preserve neutrality between rival factions, but this odd circulation of mayors between towns had not been remarked on until Louis Carolus Barré explored the texts of the *Book of justice and pleas* relating to communal government. He discovered documents confirming that this happened. A burgess of Crépy, Jean de Champbaudon, was in turn mayor of Montreuil-sur-Mer, Compiègne and Crépy. He had begun his career as a *prévôt* of Crépy in 1246 and he was *prévôt* of Paris. There were therefore, amongst the mayors of communes in the thirteenth century, some professionals. But the *Book of justice* warns us that there were burgesses who were opposed to this expedient and that they elected one of their fellow-citizens, while another party petitioned for an outsider; for the king to accept the petition the petitioners had to be twice as numerous as the electors. I do not think this procedure, which ran counter to the ambitions and interests of the already powerful oligarchies, was long in use.

Financial difficulties and a lack of men capable of preventing them or anxious to solve them equitably as a result of the growth of a selfish plutocracy and as a result of the attractions of royal office for young men of the middle classes, were in my view the most important causes of the decline of the communes during the thirteenth century. At this period, at least, the monarchy does not seem to me to have "precipitated in every possible way the decline of the communal regime", as has been claimed. It is certainly possible to cite examples of ruinous exaction, and some of the king's officers were over-zealous in curtailing communal jurisdiction; the mental attitude of the royal jurists towards the communes in the thirteenth century is known to us by the decrees of the Paris Parlement and by Chapter Fifty of Beaumanoir. *Les Olim* show the lofty impartiality with which the Parlement studied and settled cases concerning the communes. Beaumanoir's sentence about the commune which should be placed under tutelage as if it were a minor – "there is great need sometimes to help commune towns in some cases as one would a child before it has reached its majority" – has often been misapplied. What is referred to are certain occasions when the town must be defended against the fraudulent practices of mayors and *jurés*; the writer does not say that it must be deprived of its liberties.

This fiftieth chapter contains an admirable object lesson of benevolence and enlightened solicitude, addressed to "any lord who has *bonnes villes* under his care in which there is a commune". The charters must be respected, assuming they had not been allowed to fall into disuse. Consequently Beaumanoir recommends the members of the commune to make use of their franchises and, if they have to stand up for their rights, to be tried by those in the town who are established to uphold justice; only when lodging an appeal are they to have recourse to the lord "in whose jurisdiction the commune lies". The lord, for his part, must enquire every year into the state of the commune; he must know how it is governed and ensure that the rich fear "that if they commit a crime they will be severely punished, and that the poor in the said towns may earn their bread in peace".

The true spirit of St Louis breathes through these splendid pages of Beaumanoir, as it does in some decrees of the Paris Parlement. The commune must not lose its privileges, any more than it must infringe the rights of others. That is precisely the political morality advocated by St Louis. It must also be borne in mind for the correct interpretation of Beaumanoir's sentence on the creation of new communes, which may not be formed in the kingdom of France "without the king's consent, because all innovations are forbidden", that he adds later: "That is to say those innovations which are introduced in conflict with the rights of others." The king will prevent the creation of a commune, and will refrain from creating one himself, if it damages the rights of anyone else.

CHAPTER 2

Communes of the Rouen type in English Gascony in the thirteenth century

1. General characteristics

In any history of the evolution of the communes during the thirteenth century a special place must be accorded to communes of the Rouen type situated in English Gascony.

The concept of a commune employed in the king's service for the efficient defence of the town and the surrounding region can be attributed to the kings of England as dukes of Normandy and Aquitaine; after a few brief years of experience it was they who first made use of certain communes in this way. In this connection the history of the Gascon communes, which followed the pattern of the *Établissements de Rouen*, is most instructive. They grew up at the beginning or during the course of the thirteenth century, they quickly fell under the sway of wealthy families who involved them in their bloody feuds, at which point the king of England intervened. It is the fable of the oyster and the litigants.

As a conciliatory measure the king seized the office of mayor. The communes languished, subjected as they were to an oligarchy which itself owed obedience to the prince, and they lived at a slower pace from then onwards. Their history foreshadows what was later to happen in the fourteenth and fifteenth centuries in many Capetian communes. For this reason, and because they are connected both by their origins and by their constitutional development with the French communes of the thirteenth century, they must briefly occupy our attention. But it must be on the clear understanding that English Aquitaine, at this period, despite its anarchist tendencies, was firmly attached to the Plantagenet kingdom. A town such as Bordeaux was not in the slightest degree French either in heart or mind; powerful economic interests, traditions which grew stronger from generation to generation, made it during the Middle Ages, not indeed an English town, but a town loyal to the kings of England.

The distinguishing feature of the communes in the south-west, which we shall now discuss, is that they had a mayor, whereas the free towns of the south were governed by a college of consuls. This magistrate was assisted by a council of jurats; imitation of the *Établissements* of La Rochelle, that is to say of Rouen, was on occasion carried to the point at which in certain towns, Bayonne for example, there existed a college of 100 peers. Except for Bordeaux, the mayor was chosen, as at Rouen, by the prince, from a list of candidates presented by the councillors. Bémont added to Giry's rather inadequate list and enumerated the municipal constitution inspired by the *Établissements* of Rouen. He proved that west of a line drawn on the map of France from Aire-sur-Adour to Limoges, the towns of any size all had in the thirteenth century a mayor and jurats, and that they may be styled 'communes', since the word occurs in the texts. Towns on the other side of the line had a consulate.

The ebb and flow in the fortunes of the communes in the south of France was determined by the policy pursued by the Plantagenets at home and abroad. Queen Eleanor's firm clear intellect at the time of John Lackland's succession after the apathy and cowardice of John and Henry III, and finally the vigour of Edward I, successively created or renewed the political climate of the communes of Gascony. A further influence was the proximity and the attitude of the kings of France. The peace desired by St Louis and concluded in 1259 between France and England gave the English government the freedom of action it needed to subdue the communes and re-establish some semblance of order in Guyenne. But the treaty of Paris opened the doors for the king of France and his agents to claim rights of suzerainty and to receive judicial appeals.

Only three of these communes, Bayonne, Dax and the island of Oléron, may possibly antedate the accession of John Lackland. The commune of Saint-Emilion was founded at the time when John, at his mother's prompting, conceded a large number of communes in the areas threatened by Philip Augustus (1199). Bordeaux and La Réole became communes shortly afterwards, also in response to external dangers. Henry III granted a commune to the island of Ré in 1242 under the pressure of the defeats he was suffering in France. Bourg-sur-Mer (1261), Libourne (1276), and Blaye acquired a commune only very late in the day, at a time when burgesses' associations were no longer springing up in France.

2. Bordeaux

There is no trace of the most important commune of them all, Bordeaux, before 1206, when the movement created by Eleanor to resist Philip Augustus with the help of the burgess class had already slowed down. Bémont seems to have established conclusively that the inhabitants of Bordeaux formed a spontaneous association by means of the communal oath and effectively organized the government of their town in April 1206, when the king of Castile (son-in-law to Henry II Plantagenet), who claimed he was 'lord of Gascony' and was encouraged by Philip Augustus' successes, attempted to take possession of the town. Room was made in the civic body for the outsiders who had sworn the oath of fealty to the king and to "the commune of the town"; this was no doubt a reward for the help they had brought at this critical phase. John Lackland acknowledged the commune's existence, in letters of 30 April and 1 May, whereas he had hitherto addressed his letters to the *prud'hommes* of Bordeaux. In spite of the defeat of the Anglo-German coalition at Bouvines and the dethronement of John Lackland by his barons, despite the conquest of Poitou by Louis VIII in 1224, the inhabitants of Bordeaux remained loyal to the English monarchy. Henry III made them concessions: he expressly granted them a commune and an elected mayor on 30 August 1224, and on 13 July 1235 he confirmed the commune again, with all the liberties and customs appertaining to it. He made no specific provisions.

It has been noted, on comparing the *Établissements* of Rouen and the *Rolle de la vile* drawn up in 1248, that the institutions of Bordeaux were taken, in their broad outlines, from the *Établissements*. Whereas at Rouen there were 100 peers electing twelve echevins and twelve councillors, and a mayor chosen by the prince from three candidates put up by the 100 peers, at Bordeaux there were fifty jurats who elected thirty councillors, but they elected their mayor freely; the commune, without any special power, took a part in the political, administrative and judical life of Bordeaux.

This organization, which gave the prince no share in the choice of the mayor, was inadequate to maintain order, because there were in Bordeaux large wealthy families locked in bitter rivalry over the administration of the town, and also because Henry III, unable to restore strong, stable government in England, allowed anarchy to infect all his possessions on both sides of the Channel. In the early part of his reign, Bordeaux was almost an independent republic and, to defend itself, it concluded treaties of alliance with barons and with the town of La Réole. In 1222, Henry III tried in vain to forbid the town to enter into binding oaths or treaties, *sacramenta et confederationes*, with the barons and *prud'hommes* of his *bonnes villes*. Simon de Montfort, earl of Leicester, appointed royal lieutenant in Gascony in 1248, despite his energy did not succeed in disciplining the inhabitants of Bordeaux.

At this point occurred the crisis which was to be repeated fifty years later, and in a very different form, in the Capetian communes. The counsellors of the prince and lord of Gascony, Edward, sent by his father Henry III, imposed their will on the inhabitants of Bordeaux. In the statutes of 22 October 1261 they assigned to the duke the task of appointing the mayor; if the mayor administered badly or wronged a member of the commune, it was possible to appeal to the prince or his seneschal; precautions were taken against the invasion of the burgesses' ranks by outsiders; no doubt they could be made partly responsible for the welter of disturbances and crimes. Once he became king, Edward did not restore the election of the mayor to the jurats for another ten years. The dispute which broke out between his seneschal and the commune, which was brought before the Paris Parlement in 1290–91, gave him the opportunity to impose yet again a mayor of his own choosing. But in order to put an end to the humiliating summonses of the Capetian Parlement he agreed, as is well known, to hand over his territory of Aquitaine to the king of France, who then established his suzerainty over Bordeaux.

It was a harsh regime, which made the inhabitants regret Plantagenet rule. Knights from outside the town succeeded each other in the office of mayor. In the winter of 1302–03 the inhabitants of Bordeaux expelled the French. Civil war was resumed, and with it appeals to the Paris Parlement. The great war, which was to last a hundred years, put an end to appeals and civil strife alike. From 1334 the mayors of Bordeaux were all professionals. They swore fealty to the commune, but the actual principle of communal association, namely solidarity between inhabitants, was merely an empty word. The *jurade*, which shared power with the mayor, was in the hands of some thirty families, and in the fifteenth century the registers of the *jurade* contain the names of a small number of people following each other in rotation. From a total of fifty in the thirteenth century the jurats were cut down to twenty-four, then to twelve by 1375, so that Bordeaux was finally in the power of a small oligarchy who were themselves in a state of subjection. Such was the result of the ambitions and rivalries between wealthy families. In Louis XI's day, Bordeaux was in the same position as the other major towns in the kingdom.

3. Other communes in Gascony

The little commune of La Réole, about twenty-seven miles from Bordeaux, makes its appearance in history at the same time as the commune in the larger town, in about 1206–1208. Its constitution was modelled on that of its powerful ally, and its internal history was similarly disturbed by family rivalries. When Louis VIII occupied it for a few months in 1224 he exiled eight burgesses, five of whom belonged to the Piis family, who supported the English. La Réole's independence was short-lived. From 1258 onwards there was no sign of a mayor. The council, made up of the jurats and a certain number of *prud'hommes*, concerned itself with little more than the maintenance of order and with the town's economic interests: it was administered by the king's agents. The jurats and *prud'hommes* elected each other and were drawn from a small number of families.

The constitutional history of Bayonne resembles that of Bordeaux. In both towns the population was made up of ship-owners, sailors and traders; their evolution followed almost the same pattern. Was Bayonne a commune before John's reign? The vagueness of the vocabulary used in the texts does not permit of a clear-cut answer. The 'malefactors' charter' was promulgated about 1190 *suber lo segrementz dou Cosselh de Baione et de tot lo comunau* and, fifteen or twenty years later, the article of association of the Bayonne navigators was sealed with the seal held by the *proceres civitatis*; their seal was described as *sigillum sue commune*. By the mid-twelfth century there was mention of a mayor. But this term did not necessarily describe a municipal magistrate. In any case, in 1215, John Lackland, who had embarked on a struggle with the English barons, granted the inhabitants of Bayonne a commune and the *Établissements* of La Rochelle, that is, those of Rouen, while reserving "the *prévôté*, the customs and the franchises" which he was to enjoy at Bayonne and at La Rochelle.

From then on the texts relating to the town's communal character are very explicit. To acquire burgess status one had to swear an oath to the commune; the solidarity of the inhabitants was affirmed as solemnly as in the charters of the north of France: *Que tot los vesins aiudin e sien tengudz d'aiudar au vezin contra l'omi estrainh.* "All neighbours shall help and are obliged to help their neighbour against any strangers." If a stranger who has wronged a neighbour is wounded or killed by him, the commune is to stand guarantor for him.

This concession merely gave rise to further unrest in a town as turbulent as Bayonne. Two major parties were formed, which vied with each other for magistrates and power. According to Matthew Paris, one of these parties drew its support from the *plebeii civitatis*, namely the sailors and artisans, and favoured the retention of the tottering power of England. Be this as it may, the inertia of the Plantagenet monarchs plunged the town into a welter of armed attacks and murders until the earl of Leicester was appointed royal lieutenant in Gascony. The noble families, in complete disregard of the communal oath, banded together in 'brotherhoods' and their *maisnies* indulged in brigandage. In 1228 the seneschal Henry de Touberville warned King Henry III that, unless he took action, he would forfeit all authority over Bayonne. Chaos was at its height. One party, united in a brotherhood, had driven out a large number of its political opponents, and refused to recognize the king of England as its suzerain. Henry III, or rather the justiciar Hubert de Burgh, who governed during his minority, wrote on 25 June to his "dear loyal people, the mayor, jurats and commune of Bayonne," and asked them to dissolve this revolutionary brotherhood and to make restitution to the men they had banished. In 1243 Henry III introduced into Bayonne the Rouen institution of the Hundred Peers, by setting at the head of the municipal government a college of a hundred *prud'hommes* on which he relied for support. The acts of violence, the murders and the looting went on.

The energetic Simon de Montfort calmed the rebels for a time by making arrests in the anti-English party, to the great satisfaction of the knights and people, and appointed on his own initiative a mayor he could control who was at the same time royal *prévôt*. But Simon de Montfort laid down office the following year. In letters dated 29 September 1254, Henry III was again obliged to forbid the inhabitants of Bayonne to form any brotherhood or conjuration or to embark on any armed attacks. He required an oath of fealty from the noble families. This oath was sworn by 240 burgesses to his son Edward "prince and seigneur of Gascony". Edward (or rather his counsellors) continued with the repressive rule introduced by Simon de Montfort, which he was also trying to impose on the inhabitants of Bordeaux. He began by choosing outsiders as mayor; then, from 1260 onwards the office of mayor circulated amongst three relatively loyal families, the Dardis, the Meis and the Vielles. But the anarchy ravaging England, and the long absence of the prince in the Holy Land, encouraged intrigues by the opposite party and prevented the regular functioning of elections. In the fourteenth century, and particularly at its close during Richard II's reign, the burgesses on several occasions lost the right to present candidates for the office of mayor. In the fifteenth century the mayoralty became a kind of royal office.

The history of Dax is known to us only in fragmented, disconnected episodes. In the Middle Ages the town was thought to have formed a commune at a very early date. In 1219 and 1224 there are traces of the existence of a council. The inhabitants of Dax, probably obliged by force of circumstances to find themselves a leader, chose a mayor in about 1230 "on their own initiative and without the consent" of the king of England. In fact, Henry III wrote to them on 12 August 1230: "You have created from amongst yourselves a mayor, to the prejudice of our dignity and to the detriment of the town, whereas before you did not have a mayor." And he forbade them to have one. It was at this time that Henry was conducting in France what he hoped would be a victorious expedition. He failed, and in 1242 he was again defeated. Then, in 1243, he granted his *prud'hommes* of Dax the right to have a mayor and twenty jurats. Each year twenty outgoing jurats had to elect the new jurats and present to the seneschal three candidates for the office of mayor.

But at Dax, as elsewhere, the franchises granted were compromised by bloody quarrels between families attempting to fill the office of mayor by irregular procedure. This is evident from documents of 1255, 1272 and 1278. On several occasions Edward I took over the mayoral functions. The inhabitants of Dax showed him scant loyalty. When Philip the Fair occupied part of Gascony in 1294, they readily accepted French domination; their liberties were confirmed and their economic privileges increased. When the English regained possession of the town, the *mairie* was again 'confiscated' on several occasions. By the end of the Hundred Years War, Dax was an impoverished, depopulated town; Charles VII had no difficulty in reducing it to obedience.

At Saint-Émilion the elective office of mayor had been suspended from 1281 to 1312, probably because of civil strife. Edward II restored it to the inhabitants in return for a gift of fifty casks of "good wine," thereby providing them with the means to make up their differences. Saint-Émilion's constitution remained intact after the end of the Hundred Years War, and Charles VII, when he regained Gascony, confirmed the liberties of the towns in general.

The island of Oléron, possibly even in the twelfth century, formed a commune which included the whole island. One wonders whether this commune lasted very long. The only mention in the thirteenth- and fourteenth-century texts is of the mayor, the *probi homines* and the *communitas*, a word not always synonymous with *communia*. However, there is a copy of the *Établissements* of Rouen translated into French, dated 1344, and originating in Oléron: this does at least offer some indication of the political tendencies of the population.

The attraction exercised by the Rouen-type organization, which incidentally left the prince the definitive choice of the mayor and provided guarantees for him as well as for the burgesses, is still evident in the second part of the thirteenth century in the granting of a commune charter of the Rouen pattern to the inhabitants of Bourg, on the Dordogne, in 1261. Prince Edward, in making this concession, merely regularized the institutions which existed before and were inspired by those of Bordeaux. The Bourg commune was astonishingly long-lived; as late as 1668 the burgesses still possessed the right to try criminal cases in their town and suburbs.

A few years after this foundation came yet another grant, in 1270: that of the commune of Libourne, a bastide which had recently been founded by Sir Roger de Leybourne. Edward I did not immediately allow the new commune its freedom; he took over the office of mayor for a few years and entrusted the administration to an Englishman, who was the *custos ville*. In 1289 he granted the inhabitants of Libourne the right to elect their mayor; they appear to have preserved this, and they obtained the confirmation of their charter from Charles VII.

Blaye was for a long time a seigneurial town. It tried to enfranchise itself right at the end of the thirteenth century and had a mayor and jurats, but only for a short time. Louis XI endowed it with a municipality, an elective mayoralty and *jurade*, with the same prerogatives as were enjoyed by Libourne, Bourg and Saint-Émilion; in actual fact he thereby subjected it to an oligarchy whose loyalty he could count on. These municipal institutions on the Rouen model appeared to Louis XI as no more than a disguised means of wielding power.

Thus in those areas of English Aquitaine which had not been conquered by Philip Augustus and which were close to Bordeaux and the Atlantic, the history of the communes with institutions resembling those of the communes in the north of France, followed the same pattern. The king of England was so powerful a sovereign in the thirteenth century that their formation and development seem explicable only by his goodwill and his hope of finding support in them, and subsequently by the crisis abroad which absorbed the energies of the monarchy elsewhere. Their period of independence was brief. Much more quickly than in the northern communes, internal strife led straight to subjection. The institutions of mayoralty and of the *jurade*, which assured the burgesses autonomous government, also provided a convenient means of depriving them of it: the king took control of the *mairie* or mayoralty and entrusted it to outsiders, and he reduced the *jurade* to a small number of members whom he turned into privileged puppets.

We shall now examine how, by a similar but more complex process, and following a more varied pattern, the Capetian communes disappeared or lost their original character.

CHAPTER 3

Crises in the fourteenth century

1. First period. Causes of decline

The early fourteenth century was a period of disintegration for the communes. They collapsed in such rapid succession that historians have drawn the mistaken conclusion that these episodes marked the end of the French communal system. In fact they were only symptoms of a decline. What is the explanation of this?

Let us go back to the early fourteenth century and try to imagine the state of mind of the small traders, the artisans and the farmers living in town, who formed the mass of the urban population. What advantage was there for them in being organized as a commune? Their forebears had associated on oath to defend themselves and offer mutual aid, and also to obtain certain collective franchises; in order to have a charter they had been obliged to promise to pay the king a large annual due which inevitably laid a heavy burden on the municipal budget. At much less expense they could have obtained adequate franchises which would have guaranteed their modest interests, whereas the franchises they did possess worked mainly to the advantage of the wealthy, who oppressed and exploited them. In these opening years of the fourteenth century, before the disasters following in the wake of the English invasion and the formation of the great mercenary companies, the monarch's forces of order provided ample security. Certainly, the burgesses wished to be provided with a mutual insurance so as to face reverses of fortune and procure moral support during their lifetime and prayers after their death. But these needs were met by the countless confraternities which were founded in the later Middle Ages. These confraternities, which embraced industrial and commercial groups and gave them a religious life, were also societies for mutual aid. Their statutes sometimes contained the very same formulae which gave the earliest communes their character. Their founders created them "to nourish fraternal love among us" (Saint-Omer, 1344); "to nourish peace, love and charity between us and to work for the common advantage" (Arras, 1364); "for the welfare, unity and concord of the said companions as for the utility of the common good" (Béthune, 1500). They increased in number at the very time when the communes began to decrease. It is my view that this is more than two simultaneous processes at work; the prosperity of the confraternities contributed to the weakening of the communal spirit, and there was indeed in men's minds a kind of giving from one to the other.

However, alongside these pious charitable confraternities which welcomed Christians of any persuasion, another system of association grew up, which was to prove, all things considered, equally fatal to the communal principle. I refer to the craft communities, what modern historians call corporations; in the Middle Ages they called them communities or craft gilds (*corps de métier*), colleges, hansas, gilds, etc., even brotherhoods, despite the fact that they were pre-eminently professional associations; this ought not to cause the reader any surprise, in fact I have already insisted on the confusion and ambiguity of medieval vocabulary. We must remember that these *corps de métier*, some of which are very old, underwent enormous development in the thirteenth and particularly the fourteenth and fifteenth centuries, just at the time when the commune declined; nor was this process a mere coincidence.

The craft gilds differed essentially from the communes because they were professional. But they came remarkably close to them and to some extent duplicated them, in their origins, their characteristics and their privileges. They arose from a need for mutual protection, they afforded the workers greater security, defended them against the hostilities, the abuses, the rivalries of the world outside. Usually they grew up in times of peace, but occasionally after violent protests and in defiance of the ill-will displayed by the lords and the Church. Finally they wrested approval from the authorities, whether tacit or explicit.

Their members were often called *jurés* because custom frequently obliged them to swear on oath to respect the statutes. There were led by an oligarchy of employers, who ruled them so as to promote their own personal advantage. These masters held council to discuss the interests of the community and summoned the artisans to some of these meetings. These communities became legal bodies, usually possessed a legal personality, were able to own property and bring an action, and they possessed a seal. Some of them enjoyed public privilege, they took part in defending and policing the town, and in certain cases even claimed jurisdiction over their members (for example, the butchers in Paris). In their privileges and in their obligations they followed a path already traced by the communes.

There is nothing surprising in the fact that the gilds became absorbed into the municipal system, particularly in Picardy. There were towns, the entire population of which was divided between the various crafts; even the newly rich, the leisured class, fell into a category specially invented for them, namely the idle (*otiosi*). At that time certain crafts, though without ever holding an explicit monopoly of power, filled the ranks of the *échevinage*. We shall see that this was the case in Amiens at an early date: the traders in woad were accepted quite naturally as candidates for municipal office. At Beauvais, it was the money-changers and goldsmiths. In a town which had modelled itself on Amiens and had chosen Amiens to arbitrate its disputes, Abbeville, the heads of the gilds were in office at the beginning of the fourteenth century; they were called 'mayors with banners'. There were sixty-four of them, that is, four for each of the sixteen crafts in the town, from the bakers and inn-keepers to the furriers. They assisted the mayor and the twenty-four echevins. When a tax had to be levied to pay the town's debts, "they will give counsel and will help to collect the tax". They supervised the mayor's petty expenditure and were present when the outgoing mayor produced his accounts. Alongside them the 'woad mayors' fixed the scale of fines applicable to industrial misdemeanours and were present during the swearing of the oath to pay the tax, taken by all the inhabitants as they filed past the assembled echevins one by one. At Rue in Ponthieu, the 'banner mayors' appeared in 1345. Their task was to elect the mayor, from a list of four people drawn up by the echevins.

The absorption of the craft gilds into the urban administrative machine held possibilities for its renewal and invigoration; and in fact, the municipal institutions of Abbeville lasted right up to the French Revolution. But if one examines the essential communal principle, namely the association sworn by a group of inhabitants and confirmed by a charter, it becomes clear that the development of the craft gilds was not at all conducive to its preservation. What was the point of all the oath-taking? Surely everyone could count on help in case of need from the members of his gild brotherhood. What was the use of a commune charter? Were not the gilds' statutes enough? Besides, it was not only certain towns with a commune charter which could count on the collaboration of the gilds. This collaboration was fundamental in the administration of large towns, including the capital of the kingdom, which were not communes. This was yet another way of obscuring the specific characteristics which differentiated the communes from other towns; here again there was a tendency to confuse them with the other *bonnes villes.*

And so the decline of the communes was made inevitable by rival forces called into play by social progress. They had, without realizing it, fallen victim to a slowly developing malady the outcome of which lay in the distant future and varied considerably according to circumstance. The sudden collapse of some of them, in the first half of the fourteenth century, had more proximate causes.

The conditions in which the communes found themselves when Beaumanoir was writing changed, sometimes for the worse. The monarchy was short of money, which made its behaviour harsh and exacting. The finances of the communes were disorganized by the burdensome fines imposed by the Parlement. The officials of the *curia regis* and the royal *baillis* became meddlesome, and could now even be termed hostile; gone was their wish to be the benevolent guardians of children "of a tender age". For example, they invented and applied the theory that no commune existed if there were no charter: the case of Chelles, which I have cited, was not unique. The lords, too, in proportion as they themselves suffered molestation at the hands of the royal officials, became correspondingly more meddlesome and surly towards their subjects, and jurisdictional disputes became frequent. But the members of the commune, for reasons I have indicated, were less and less able to withstand the jurists ranged against them, or the litigants who were skilled at obtaining royal favours. The Saint-Quentin archives contain a most curious letter from a certain cleric called Jean de Ribemont, addressed, during the reign of Philip the Fair, to the mayor and *jurés* of the town. He says he is no longer prepared to be involved in their affairs; they will shortly drain the cup of confusion. They imagine that, in their disputes with the churches of Saint-Quentin, they can succeed by entrusting their cause to that loud-mouthed Gobert, the draper: "And so you think you can win by bawling and shouting, but this is not so, for you are dealing the people who enjoy all the favour of the court".

In 1391 the king authorized the Hundred Peers of Angoulême to appoint the mayor directly, without consulting the other inhabitants, since there were "so few people sufficiently skilled to participate in the government of the said town"; his seneschal told him the inhabitants were "simple folk, who are not wise or discreet enough to arrange such a matter". In the view of the Hundred Peers, it would be necessary to call on the royal officers or licentiates in law from outside, who were in actual fact debarred from becoming mayor. At Abbeville, and undoubtedly in many other communes, there were echevins who could neither read nor write. The difficulty of finding echevins merely increased the danger that municipal office would be monopolized by specific families; this scandal grew worse with the passage of time.

It is hardly surprising that indifference gradually dissolved the communal bonds. Other causes have been adduced. A little later in the reign of John the Good, the horrors of the Hundred Years' War were unleashed upon France; it has been claimed that this war "discouraged the communal movement". I cannot subscribe to this view. Far from putting an end to the traditions of urban independence, the English invasions and the devastation wrought by the Great Companies would have stimulated the 'communal movement' if such a thing had been possible. Paul Viollet has pointed out that the commissions of burgesses in charge of fortifications sometimes developed into *corps de ville*, and that, particularly on the banks of the Loire, certain towns owed their late emancipation to the Hundred Years War. He even wondered "whether several of our communes date from the ill-fated reigns of Philip VI and John the Good". But he bases his remarks on a decree of 1347 whereby Philip VI granted municipal liberties to the burgesses of Mâcon, to thank them for their help, and he has ignored this reservation, which runs counter to his argument: "however, it is not our intention that on this account they should have or be obliged to have any other body or commune or ordinary jurisdiction." The exigencies of war gave rise to organs of defence, increased the number of towns with echevins, but did not restore vigour to a decaying institution, and it was only exceptionally that in certain threatened localities, as we shall see, there was a revival of one or two older communes of the military type.

To sum up, the French communes, two centuries after their birth, were suffering from an internal malady which developed more or less slowly; the Hundred Years War affected them neither for good nor for ill.

2. Disappearance of communes

It was before the break between the kings of France and England that some communes began to disband of their own accord. Their financial situation was in most cases, if not the underlying psychological reason, at least the immediate cause of their suicide.

St Louis could not but be aware of the financial embarrassment of his communes and he had tried to remedy the situation. In 1260 thirty or more *villes de commune*, belonging to the Paris and north-east region, towns of the royal domain or episcopal walled towns subject to royal tutelage, like Noyon or Beauvais, had been requested to give an account of their revenues and expenses. In 1262 St Louis prescribed that henceforward the communes of 'France' and Normandy should present their accounts in this way each year, "to the officials of the king in charge of accounts," on 17 November, after the renewal of their municipality. Absorbed in his pious dreams of crusades and peace at any price between Christians he made the municipal magistrates responsible for their indebtedness, and appeared unaware that his reign marked the beginning of the system of permanent deficit, both for the monarchy and for the collectivities which supported it. From 1248 to 1260 he levied six taxes on the towns for his crusade and for the crushing peace treaty with the king of England.

The 1262 ordinances produced little effect. The date, 29 October, which the king had hoped to fix for the renewal of municipalities, was observed only in rare instances. Some years after St Louis' death the habit of producing accounts ceased.

Noyon had been one of the towns hardest pressed by the unreasonable demands of the king and his family. In 1278 the commune, met together in general assembly, asked King Philip the Bold to authorize it to pay its debts, which amounted to 16,000 *livres*; until the debts had been settled, a tax of 6,000 *livres*, apportioned by "the man whom the king shall appoint" was to be raised annually. Not until 1291 did the Parlement give judgement; it prescribed partial bankruptcy, on the pretext that the creditors had made usurious loans; it also inflicted harsh treatment on the administrators who, on investigation, were found responsible for the wrong done to the 'commune' by default, malice and trickery: their property was to be confiscated and handed over to the creditors. In 1333 the liquidation of these debts, which had been delayed by a disastrous fire which destroyed the town, was still not complete. On these terms Noyon retained the commune, which it kept until 1789. But the bishop had taken advantage of this crisis to interfere in the town's affairs and regain ancient rights which had lapsed. Thus Noyon forfeited part of its independence and began once again to fall into debt.

In the present state of our knowledge, and if one excepts the special case of the town of Corbie which we shall examine later, the town of Sens seems to have been the earliest to make a voluntary sacrifice of its charter.

A certain number of inhabitants complained to King Louis X of the bad administration of the mayor and *jurés* and asked for the commune to be abolished. The revenues of the town were sparse and it had to pay an annual "gift to the king" promised years before to Philip Augustus, as well as an "abbot's fine" imposed as a perpetual punishment for the murder of the abbot of Saint-Pierre-le-Vif in 1147. A fragment of an account found by Duplès-Agier shows that in 1259 "the town owed the king for his gift and its fine 1,065 *livres*, 13 *sous*, 4 *deniers*"; the king's gift, which could be increased if necessary, sometimes amounted to 2,000 *livres*. In the reign of Philip the Fair the exactions of the royal officials, the judicial fines, had become so burdensome that the wealthy made certain of withholding their contribution by ceasing to belong to the commune. By order of Louis X, the *bailli* called together the inhabitants, who voted for the abolition of the commune, despite a minority supported by the mayor, who were in favour of retaining it. A *prévôt* replaced the mayor and took charge of the government of the town. After some hesitation, the Paris Parlement pronounced the suppression of the commune on 14 February 1318.

In April 1318 the same thing happened to the Champagne federation of Bourbonne, Chantemerle and neighbouring villages. These villagers could no longer sustain the annual burden of 170 *livres tournois* which they had been paying ever since their commune was founded a very long time ago; the federation was in debt. The king agreed to abolish the commune and to cancel the debt, and resumed his judicial functions together with the revenues; he restored the franchises which the inhabitants had enjoyed before they had a commune.

The following year the inhabitants of Compiègne also requested the abolition of their commune, which was granted them by King Philip the Tall. They were probably weary of the hostility shown to their town by the Parlement, because of its constant disputes with the abbey of St Cornelius. The king drew up rules for the liquidation of the debts and left to the burgesses the task of maintaining the fortifications and administering the property held in common: they were to elect four *attournés* for this purpose.

In 1320 the inhabitants of Meulan obtained from Philip, count of Evreux, the abolition of their commune and all the expenses and debts that went with it, because the mayor and echevins, in order to "uphold the rights and privileges of this commune" had "heavily burdened and damaged it with taxes, levies, and contributions". Prevotal justice was re-established, with right of appeal to the count's bailiff. The inhabitants were perfectly free to meet to discuss their affairs, without being accused of '*taqueham*', that is, conspiracy, but the bell could be rung only by order of the lord's officers.

The history of the abolition of the Senlis commune has been set out in full detail by the meticulous Flammermont. He tells us of a mayor who forgot to pay his tax for several consecutive years; he tells us of municipal spendthrifts who were in the habit of entering in the debit column of their accounts sums they had not paid, and of failing to enter in the credit column sums they had received. Friends and relatives did not interfere. They knew that when they themselves came to power they would be able to rely on the complicity of the embezzlers they had encouraged. Past and future mayors alike speculated, obtaining contracts at knock-down prices, and paralysing trade by introducing protectionist measures. Justice was dispensed with such partiality that almost every year the *bailli* or the Paris Parlement reversed decisions and on that account imposed fines amounting to 400 or 500 *livres*: but it was the town, not the erring magistrate, who paid. The town was faced with the simultaneous burdens of running expenses, the annual rents demanded by the king and the former lords of the town for the purchase of their rights, the heavy interest on borrowed money, life interest on the town hall, the expenses of endless law suits and fines on account of reversed decisions, etc. The ordinary revenues brought in only tiny resources, and extraordinary taxes had to be levied; only part of these ever reached the municipal treasury. The wealthy citizens forgot to pay, and so fresh loans were contracted and gradually the town was driven to bankruptcy.

The Parlement, at the request of the common people, ordered an enquiry. The commissioners noted that there was dangerous discussion between high and low, that "the commune was completely useless and damaging to the state and all the public affairs of the town," and that the removal of the mayor, the echevins and the *jurés* was desired by all the inhabitants, "with the exception of a small number who had in the past been in charge of the town and administered it badly". Consequently the Parlement, in a decree of 16 February 1320, pronounced the abolition of the commune. The inhabitants of Senlis were treated with unusual severity. The king confiscated all the property and all the revenues of the commune, leaving to the inhabitants the ordinary and extraordinary expenses, including the liquidation of debts; he even obliged them to embark on ruinous law-suits. They had not even the right to have their debtors arrested or to ring the bells in case of fire. The burgesses, overwhelmed with taxes, allowed themselves to be imprisoned, then on their release abandoned their property. It took several years before this harsh treatment was mitigated.

There was no rich, tyrannical aristocracy at Soissons, a little farming community which made its living from the fruits of the earth. The causes of its financial downfall are obscure. The probable explanation is that its magistrates were incompetent and that the fines imposed by the gens du roi finally unbalanced the budget. Whatever the reason, the inhabitants complained to the king in 1325 that they could not meet their expenses. They had no course left, they said, but to leave town "like paupers and beggars". On 1 November the mayor handed over the running of affairs to a prévôt. The king acknowledged that the inhabitants deserved, on losing their commune, to keep their franchises. Charles VI declared in 1411: "The commune possessed by the inhabitants of our town of Soissons was restored by them to us or to our predecessors without any question of forfeiture." Philip VI, in his 'liberal' ordinances of 1341, granted the inhabitants of Soissons, the right to elect a mayor, four echevin governors, a treasurer and an attorney (procureur), to try their own law-suits, and in 1342 the right to assemble once a week. The prévôt retained supervision of the municipal finances.

Crépy-en-Valois, like Soissons, did not suffer from the disputes of two hostile factions, but was simply a commune heavily in debt and living off borrowed funds, a town where all that remained was a "small impoverished company of inhabitants"; the richer families preferred to settle elsewhere rather than pay extortionate taxes or take the responsibility of trying to remedy the deficit. The charter granting a commune to Crépy had been largely copied from that of Senlis: they were neighbouring towns. But the example of Senlis and its disastrous liquidation held little encouragement for the people of Crépy. They waited until their count, Philip of Valois, ascended the French throne, before requesting the suppression of their commune. They asked for it immediately after his accession because they hoped to obtain favourable conditions and retain their principal franchises. The gens du roi held somewhat acrimonious discussions with them about the redemption of the perpetual rent of 407 livres which the commune owed the king, and insisted on retaining any sum which might exceed the revenues handed over by the town. But the burgesses were allowed to retain the guarantees against arbitrary action and abuses, and they were glad to be relieved of their financial worries. The royal prévôt was instructed to liquidate the debts and had to compel all the burgesses to contribute to the common expenses (1329).

A few years later came the disappearance of the Provins commune, the most vigorous of the communes in Champagne, the one which had the widest franchises and displayed the greatest energy in defending them: it had a famous fair, in which its cloth industry found an assured outlet, and it continued to flourish throughout the period of prosperity enjoyed by the Champagne fairs. It ranked as one of the most populous communes in France, including its *vilois*, that is to say, the eight surrounding villages which formed part of the commune. If we were to consult a document of the mid-fourteenth century (which will be discussed later), namely the list containing the voters' names, in a general assembly of vital importance, which it was in the inhabitants' interest to attend, we should find that there were at least five to six thousand souls within the walls of Provins and three or four thousand in the *vilois*.

The reigns of Philip the Bold and Philip the Fair saw the beginning of the commercial decline of Provins. The working population was dissatisfied and restless, and in 1279 they rose up when fresh taxes were imposed; they probably accused the rich burgesses in power of an unfair distribution of tax burdens: the mayor Guillaume Pentecoste was murdered and the houses of several *jurés* were ransacked. Jean de Brienne, grand cup-bearer of France, was appointed to put down the uprising. The ringleaders were hanged and crushing fines were imposed on the town; the drapers' community alone paid 4,000 *livres*. The commune was abolished, but it was re-established as early as 1281. In the fourteenth century, Provins was fated to undergo further exactions by the king's tax collectors and to suffer brutal harassment by the *gens du roi*, war and famine. The economic and social uncertainty found expression in acts of popular sedition in 1310, 1324 and 1349. In 1349 the monastery of Saint-Ayoul was sacked by the mob. It is probable that the second suppression of the commune, the precise date of which is unknown, had taken place by this time. This was apparently caused by class hatred, the town's progressive indebtedness, and the ruthlessness with which the royal *prévôt* destroyed the franchises.

Longnon has published the list of grievances which the *prud'hommes* of Provins had brought before the king some years previously. The document bears no date. It refers to the complaints presented in Paris in 1320 and the town accounts mention the mayor's travelling expenses when he set out on 26 February 1320 to complain to the king "about various damage, harm, and injuries which Miles Tassins and Jacques de Joy, *prévôts* of Provins, were causing the commune". In particular, the *prévôts* tried to forbid the magistrates of Provins from exercising their judicial rights, to prevent the nobles and the clergy from responding to summonses issued by the magistrates, and three times they pulled down the *loge* in which the urban court of justice sat. They confiscated the bread from the burgesses' bread-bins under the pretext that the grain had not been ground in the lord's mill or the bread baked in his oven. They sent one of their sergeants, who had a glib tongue, to spread propaganda in the town, "to tell the people to leave the commune, because it was worthless, and to change to a *prévôté* ". The petitioners ended with these words: "Know, Sire, truly before God, and the *prud'hommes* of this town would be very amazed, very put out and very alarmed, if they were deprived of what they have held and what you have given them."

The king waited until the majority of the inhabitants had requested the abolition of the commune, and one day, following a series of events which are unknown to us, he asked them to come to a decision in a general assembly. Bourquelot discovered the verbatim accounts: 2,701 people voted. 156 people, of whom 140 were from Provins and 16 from the village of Rouilly, declared that they wished to remain under the administration of mayors and echevins; the rest, 2,545 people, made up of 1,601 from Provins and 944 from the villages, declared they wished to be "outside the government of mayors and echevins and to be governed by the king alone". The oligarchy was defeated, and the commune was suppressed. From 1344, there is no further mention of a mayor, and in a document dated 1356 there is an allusion to the "time when there used to be a mayor in Provins". The history of Provins proves conclusively that the selfishness and the bad administration of the capitalist burgess class contributed greatly to the success of the intrigues of the royal officers and to the decline of the commune.

It was not only incompetent administrators, financial embarrassment and crushing taxes, but also grinding poverty and depopulation which certain towns had to suffer when the English and the mercenaries laid waste the soil of France. The reign of John the Good and the early years of Charles V's reign brought poverty and depopulation into prosperous areas like the Vermandois and the Beauvaisis. In 1370 the inhabitants of La Neuville-Roy in the diocese of Beauvais went and informed the king that their commune, which was administered according to the customs of Senlis, could no longer pay the receiver of the Vermandois the 100 *livres* it was obliged to pay annually: the war had ruined it. It had only thirty poor labourer's dwellings instead of 300, and most of the properties were deserted. The king decided that the commune should be abolished, and that the inhabitants, ruled now by a *prévôt*, should be released from their debt; he commanded the officials of the *chambre des comptes* in Paris to "remove and delete the said inhabitants from the registers of the *chambre des comptes*, where they were entered and registered".

In January 1373 Roye-en-Vermandois suffered the same fate. Ever since "the granting or long-standing toleration" of a commune, the king had drawn from it an annual income of 111 *livres* 16 *sols parisis*, quite apart from the *cens*, the revenues, and "great profits and emoluments both in justice and in *aides*". But enemies had burned down the town, and it was now practically deserted. In order to rebuild and repopulate it, the king declared, at the request of the inhabitants, that they should no longer use "the authority of the commune, legal or other rights, but they shall remain plain inhabitants, our subjects in a *prévôté*".

In most of the towns or large villages we have been discussing the greater part of the population had deserved and requested the abolition of the commune. The case of the suppression of the Corbie commune, which went back to 1310, was more complex, in that the inhabitants were the victims of a trick. The commune had been granted by Louis the Fat in 1123, at the unanimous request of all classes of inhabitants. The monks of the famous abbey probably found it to their advantage to allow the people to become more solidly organized so as to defend the town. The burgesses obtained quite extensive privileges during the thirteenth century, in particular 'high' justice, with the power to pronounce banishment and condemn to death anyone except the monks of the abbey. But the abbot stoutly defended his title of "sire of the town of Corbie" holding, in countship and baronage for the king's service, "the town and the lordship, lands, meadows, lakes, rivers, woods, fiefs, sub-fiefs, homages, liege men, lordships and many other things". From the reigns of Louis VII and Philip Augustus, and in spite of the charter granted and maintained by Philip Augustus, disputes were constant. The commissioners of the king and the Parlement intervened, enlarged on and interpreted the texts, but to no avail. The perusal of their reports and their sentences gives one a fair idea of the ceaseless chicanery, encroachments, and acts of violence, which made life intolerable for monks and townsfolk alike. There were unending disputes over jurisdiction and the carrying out of sentences, arrests, seizure of goods, policing of markets and taverns, rights of use, fortifications, taxes, etc. In 1225 the monks decided to fortify the monastery by digging moats; the burgesses filled in the moats. In 1238 the burgesses opposed the building of a fortress at Fouilloy, a dependency of the monks, laid hands on the abbot and were consequently excommunicated by the pope. In 1255 they formed a confederation under the command of fourteen captains, and in three years they levied a tax of 9,000 *livres* to meet pressing needs, without the abbot's permission. In 1277 and in 1307 there occurred fresh acts of violence. For a considerable time, at least, the Paris Parlement seems to have tried to be fair; it often condemned the town to pay heavy fines, but when the monks behaved badly the Parlement refused to allocate them damages for the reprisals they had suffered.

It was financial deficit which caused the defeat of the burgesses of Corbie. The revenues of the commune were negligible, and it was constantly reduced to borrowing; the monks refused to impose a tariff on merchandise on the pretext that it would cut their profits by driving traders away from the town. The surly tone of the methods adopted by the proctor of the abbey demonstrates vividly the animosity which set the monks and inhabitants of Corbie at loggerheads with each other. The burgesses, so the proctor asserted, maintained that they would be obliged to beg, unless they received help soon. He denied this. They could perfectly well pay their debts out of their normal resources. The taxpayers "are rich and well-off, quite accustomed to paying their taxes in the normal way, without going begging and without destroying their commune, for they are richer than they have been before".

The inhabitants thought they could transfer the commune, with its landed property and its legal rights, "to the king and to royal law", and they did so in 1310. The abbot did not interfere, but he requested the king to unite the possessions and rights of the commune, not to his domain but to the abbey's domain, in exchange for which the abbot would cede him the villages of Wailly and La Royère, and a sum of 6,000 *livres*; peace would at last return to the monastery once the commune was abolished. The king agreed. He appointed two commissioners, who called together the monks and the inhabitants, informed them of the exchange accepted by the king, and possessed the abbot of the commune, by handing over to him the key of the gates, the fortifications, the prisons and the belfry. "Immediately", the commissioners tell us in their account of what happened, "the monks protested in our presence that they did not wish the commune to continue at Corbie and that they revoked it completely and expressly, so far as they were concerned". They removed the clappers from the bells, and the belfry was pulled down shortly afterwards.

The inhabitants of Corbie fell once again under the sway of the monks, although they had hoped to be ruled by a royal *prévôt* who would assume the task of liquidating their debts. They had been tricked, and it was not long before they felt the full effects of their honesty. The abbot imposed crushing fines on them, refused to entrust notables of the town with the task of trying law-suits between inhabitants, and delayed eleven years before allowing a liquidation tax. In 1356 the inhabitants rose up, took the law into their own hands, and elected twelve of their number "for the preservation of the liberties and rights of the town". The king re-established the abbot's authority. Two years later, in the middle of a peasant uprising, the abbot took fright and deserted Corbie; the inhabitants, although they had neither "corporate body, college, commune, bell nor seal, but were single individuals", appointed a captain to rule them, had a town seal engraved, and dug earthworks on abbey land; but this liberation attempt failed after six months, and the inhabitants were obliged to pay the abbot damages.

Scarcely had they abandoned their sworn association of two centuries' standing than they longed for it back and tried to regain their independence. The history of their communal life and the ultimate victory of the Corbie monks is a striking example of the antipathies which, in certain towns, divided the burgesses from the clergy, and of the difficulty experienced by the burgesses of a small town in matching their wits against an ecclesiastical overlord.

Laon succumbed in the same way, after a long resistance. In this case the issue was an episcopal authority. At the end of the thirteenth century violent disputes arose between the burgesses on the one hand and the clergy and nobility on the other. In 1295 the inhabitants, after ringing the bells and locking the gates of the town, invaded the cathedral church and dragged out one of the clergy and some nobles who had taken sanctuary inside to escape their fury; they mishandled one of the nobles so cruelly that he died. The echevins, the *jurés*, the sergeants of the commune, all watched these acts of violence without uttering a word of protest. After an enquiry, the royal court pronounced the abolition of the commune, in terms which have already been quoted. But this decree was not implemented and the commune was re-established in 1297 "only for as long as it shall please the king to maintain it". The disturbances went on, and at the urgent request of the bishop and chapter a decree of the Paris Parlement of 13 March 1321 abolished the commune for the second time. In letters written during July 1322, King Charles IV, to avoid, he said, the scandals and dangers threatening the church and the inhabitants, abolished the commune in perpetuity and transferred the rights of jurisdiction and of burgesses' association to the *prévôté*. In 1328, on Philip VI's accession, the former *communiers* requested that their commune should be restored permanently. The bishop protested: the 1322 decree had been pronounced because of "excesses inhumanly committed in the mother church of Laon" and because of "several appalling injuries, inflicted on the persons of their prelate": moreover many inhabitants thought there was no advantage "in having a commune".

The king could not go back on what had been decided. The burgesses objected that every satisfaction had been given to the church, both by restitution and repayment of fines and by processions in which they had participated; lastly, "all those persons who had been present at the aforesaid evil deeds were dead". The king replied that he had the right to establish a commune in the town any time he wished, and he enjoined perpetual silence on the bishop and chapter. He added that he would send "good people" to examine whether the commune would do more harm than good. At this point the bishop resorted to extreme measures. He convinced Philip VI by means of high-sounding arguments and the king decided there would never again be a commune instituted at Laon. In letters of March 1332–1333 he settled the administration of the town and fixed in detail the rights of the bishop of Laon. Peace was slow to return. The burgesses brought down anathema on their heads and paid scant heed to the fact: in 1363 the dauphin Charles ordered the *bailli* of Vermandois to oblige these excommunicates, who were "rich and plentifully endowed", to take absolution. In the fifteenth century there was no further question of a commune at Laon. Here as at Corbie, but with less speed, the Church had got the better of the commune.

Tournai was in a much more encouraging situation. The municipal life of this commune weathered many storms, finding a guarantee in its political importance which increased steadily in the fourteenth and fifteenth centuries because of its geographical situation and its links with the French Crown. No abolition of their commune inflicted on the inhabitants of Tournai could be anything but temporary. The kings were fond of reminding the inhabitants how highly they regarded "the situation of their town which is sited on the confines of the kingdom looking onto the Empire, and also "the great, notable and welcome services" of its inhabitants who were "always found to be faithful and loyal to the Crown of France". It was "one of the most notable towns in the kingdom, which in former times was better built, with the finest of houses, and the inhabitants were rich and comfortable". We have already had occasion to say that they enjoyed exceptional privileges. The kings of the fourteenth and fifteenth centuries specified that the magistrates of Tournai, *prévôts*, *jurés*, echevins and inspectors (*esgardeurs*) were "nobly provided with corporate body, law and commune", and had in the town

and its suburb "all justice and suzerainty, high, middle and low, with all
the profits and revenues of the same justice and of the domain of the said
town and suburb, in the jurisdiction and sovereignty of the court of
Parlement, without intermediary" and without being obliged to plead
anywhere else but in the Parlement.

The inhabitants of Tournai were tempted on several occasions to
abuse their privileges, and from the very outset the king had to intervene
to defend the church of Tournai. On the other hand, although the
magistrates' offices were renewed annually, they remained in the hands of
a burgess aristocracy. As a result of excesses and violations of the king's
safe-conduct a sentence passed on 3 July 1332 by the Parlement of Paris
deprived the inhabitants of Tournai, for ever, of "corporate body, college
échevinage, bells and commune", but a few months later, in May 1333, at
the urgent request of the inhabitants, governed since olden times in a
commune and ever loyal subjects, Philip VI granted them a commune
once again; in August 1340 he confirmed his decision and defined the
powers of the magistrates. Letters of non-prejudice granted on 13
October to the bishop and chapter testify to the fears of the clergy. The
spirited defence of the town, when it was besieged by Edward III, placed
it in a favourable position.

During Charles V's reign, the government of the aristocracy
displeased the common people once again. The king, who judged that the
great dissensions and discords between the middle and lesser burgesses
were putting Tournai "on the road to ruin and destruction", that the said
burgesses "could not agree together so long as they had a corporate body
and a commune", and considering moreover that many walled cities and
towns in the kingdom were governed by the king's officers, to their
greater advantage, without being rent by internal strife, decided that the
burgesses of Tournai should no longer possess a corporate body and
commune, should cease to be self-governing, and should cease to exercise
any authority at Tournai.

In 1370 the inhabitants, affirming their desire for peace, requested the
restitution of their liberties, and Charles V, on enquiry, restored them in
February 1371. In his letters he declared that when he had removed their
liberties his aim had been to put the inhabitants to the test, and to give
them back their law, estate and commune, as soon as he saw that harmony
was restored. However, the liberties of the town did suffer some harm. To
win back all their commune rights, with all justice and suzerainty both
high and low, the inhabitants of Tournai paid Charles VI, in 1383, over

and above a sum of 6,000 francs to celebrate his accession, a further sum of 12,000 francs, and undertook to provide aid amounting to 6,000 *livres tournois* annually. In return for these payments he promised that the law obtaining in Tournai would not suffer further modification and that its customs would be confirmed, and a royal *bailli* would be established for Tournai, which had hitherto formed part of the *bailliage* of Vermandois. The Tournai commune continued to exist, and remained loyal to the king of France, even when he was no more than the 'king of Bourges'.

Saint-Quentin suffered a similar fate to that of Tournai, and profited by an indulgence which was mainly inspired by its strategic situation. The king needed burgesses to defend France. We have already seen in what circumstances and with what dogged perseverance the inhabitants had, as early as the twelfth century, won their independence. In the thirteenth century, although Philip Augustus' charter had restricted their liberties, the administration of justice was in the hands of municipal magistrates, as a result of the fusion of the old *échevinage*, seigneurial in origin, with the urban law-court. Philip Augustus had kept the administration of higher justice for himself, but the *bailli* and *prévôt* could not prevent encroachment by the *jurés*, with strong support from the echevins. The chapter and the abbey were exposed to acts of violence. In 1213 the mayor, Robert Cat-Nose, was banished by the king for leading a rebellion against the chapter. The uprising of 1240 must have been serious, because the town had to pay 10,000 *livres* in fines. But the situation did not become really dangerous for the commune until the reign of Philip the Fair, when levies of men and money incensed the population: in 1293 the town was punished with a fine of 2,000 *livres* for having put a royal castellan in irons; two years later a tax levy provoked a rebellion. In 1299 the town clashed violently with the archbishop of Rheims; in 1311 the abbey of Saint-Quentin-en-l'Isle was attacked. From that moment the king's officers awaited their opportunity to request the suppression of the commune. Encroachments on the bailliff's jurisdiction furnished a suitable pretext. The Paris Parlement, in a decree of 23 December 1317, suspended the commune of Saint-Quentin. As a result, a certain number of burgesses left the town, and the upkeep of roads and fortresses was neglected. King Charles VI, fearing the town "might grow still worse and diminish further", re-established the commune with the one requirement of a "pecuniary punishment" of 6,000 *livres tournois*.

The town was prosperous and in a reasonably sound financial position when the Hundred Years War broke out. Philip VI showed the town kindness, which was no doubt partly attributable to political considerations, but also to a personal inclination, it would seem, to treat the burgesses well. In 1346 he solemnly recognized that the inhabitants of Saint-Quentin enjoyed the right to administer justice which they had arrogated to themselves and which the *bailli* and *prévôt* had refused to admit. But with the reign of John the Good the decline really set in. In 1352 the royal proctor requested the Parlement to revoke the letters granted by Philip VI; he accused the burgesses of deceiving the king by laying before him a false interpretation of Philip Augustus' charter. The Parlement granted the *procureur's* request, revoked the letters of 1346, and ordered the mayor and *jurés* to return them to him. He gave a detailed definition of their rights. Finally he condemned the town to pay a fine of 10,000 *livres tournois*. The Vermandois was ruined by war and Saint-Quentin was unable to pay such a sum; it had to be reduced by half. But from that time on the door was open to the despotism of the royal officers and to the cupidity of the *prévôt* tax farmer, and the disasters which marked the end of John the Good's reign utterly broke the spirit of the already disheartened population.

In the fourteenth century when a French commune passed to the suzerainty of the king of England, it was a simple matter, it would seem, to defend its autonomy by having recourse to the protection of the king of France, his supreme suzerain. This was the hope cherished by the inhabitants of Abbeville when the last of the Plantagenets became, by marriage, counts of Ponthieu. But in fact their commune almost received its death blow. It was suspended on several occasions. In 1307 the mayor and two echevins were accused of peculation by a section of the magistrates and by the population. The seneschal, acting on behalf of the count, took the *échevinage* and the commune under his control and appointed a governor to administer the town. The mayor and echevins removed from office placed themselves under the protection of the king of France. We have insufficient documentation of this affair, which went on for several years. But we do possess a curious document relating to it, reporting a dialogue between the mayor and echevins on the one hand and the *bailli* and recently appointed governor on the other. The placid obstinacy and mocking effrontery of these Picard burgesses are vividly revealed. The officers who had been dismissed had continued to administer Abbeville. The *bailli* ordered them to give up the keys and the archives and to obey the governor henceforward in all matters; the governor, after having the letters read aloud which confirmed him in office, said to them:

"My lords, despite the fact that you have been prohibited and suspended you have administered and you still continue to exercise jurisdiction over this town, wherefore I command you ... to imprison yourselves in the belfry, until you have set right your misdemeanour."

And they asked: "When will that be? Before supper or after?"

And the governor replied: "It is now, without delay, that I command you to do it."

Then they replied: "We know very well what we should do."

And the governor said: "If you do what you should, you will obey my orders."

And they said all the time: "We shall do what we have to do." And they refused to do or reply anything else. And the *bailli* and the governors adjourned for a fortnight the case of those who said they were mayor and echevins.

In 1326–27 the magistrates and the inhabitants, both nobles and commoners, were accused of refusing to obey the countess Isabel, queen of England, or her son Edward, of former illegal associations against them, of levying taxes without permissiion and of wasting the money. The commune was suspended. The mayor and echevins lodged an appeal with the Paris Parlement, called a general assembly and forbade the inhabitants to obey the countess and her officers. Finally, the inhabitants of Abbeville were obliged to give in. They had relied too much on the political crisis which had temporarily weakened the English government.

In the examples we have just examined the immediate causes of the suspension of the commune in the fourteenth century were revolts provoked by royal taxes, or disputes between the *gens du roi* and the Church, or internal dissension. It resumed its existence after paying a ransom or else it invoked to good effect its loyalty and the services it rendered to the king. In the case of Falaise and Péronne the reasons for the suspension of the commune are not clear. In the reign of Philip the Fair the commune of Falaise was confiscated "because of countless excesses and injustices perpetrated by the mayor and burgesses", then restored in exchange for a payment of 1,400 *sols tournois*. In the reign of Charles V the inhabitants of Péronne, no doubt fearing a trick which would hand them over to the English, refused to allow the duke of Orléans or the count of Eu to enter their town, and drove back their escort; the commune "was taken away and abolished" but on 28 January 1369 it was restored.

It also happened that the lord of a town suspended the functions of the communal magistrature with the aim of reforming a constitution which conferred too great a power on the wealthier burgesses. For example, in 1305 the *commun* of Saint-Omer was driven beyond endurance by the selfishness of the wealthy families who monopolized all the municipal offices and turned them to their own advantage; the *bailli* of Hesdin had to intervene and both sides agreed to entrust the countess of Artois with the task of introducing a reform. She took over the town's administration and made a provisional choice of echevins. The statute of 23 May 1306 modified the electoral system and introduced precautionary measures to combat the monopoly of offices, but the rule governing the conditions of eligibility reserved the *échevinage* for "the most loyal and the wisest burgesses", possessing a fortune of at least 500 *livres tournois*. Disturbances flared up again immediately and the knights, supported by the burgess militia of Arras, had to restore order. In August there was a fresh uprising, again followed by military intervention. Eventually peace was restored by means of a fine and the handing over of hostages. The countess reserved for herself and her successors the right to "reform the status of the town, to correct and put right things that go wrong". But the commune was not abolished.

Similarly, in 1319, the Countess Mahaut listened to the protests of "the greater part of the *commun* (sic) of the town" of Bapaume against the election of the mayor and the report of the expenses of his predecessor, who had wasted the t)wn's money on travelling. Until she knew the result of the enquiry, she entrusted the conduct of affairs to four governors. In 1372, in view of the complaints produced against the way the mayor and *jurés* of Hesdin were embezzling money, and also in view of the hatred existing between the notables themselves, the Countess Marguerite amended the administration and cut down the number of *jurés*; while this was going on she naturally assumed the conduct of affairs herself.

But the most serious and the most characteristic events of seigneurial intervention in Artois were the scandals at Arras and the tutelage imposed by the counts on the aristocracy of echevins, whose intrigues and tyranny were recounted in an earlier chapter. In 1285 when the count of Artois, Robert II, was away in Sicily, the inhabitants of Arras rebelled, and the echevins were fortunate to escape with their lives. The trial which took place on the count's return revealed gross abuses. In 1302, the very year when Mahaut succeeded Robert II, a commission of twenty-four burgesses was set up to supervise the echevins' administration, and it took its task seriously. An enquiry instituted in 1305 into the intrigues of the most notorious capitalist of Arras, Matthew Lanstier, and an adventurer who had recently settled in the town, John Beauparisis, reveals a population terrorized by the daring of these two men. Matthew Lanstier, for example, pocketed annuities from the town due to non-existent persons, made certain that an assassin went unpunished, etc. We do not know the outcome of the 1305 trial, but certainly the town's finances were reorganized. But we shall see that, despite the zeal displayed by the Twenty-Four, popular hatred for the burgess dynasties persisted, and in the reign of John the Good they were nearly swept away in a whirlwind.

3. Second period. Burgess revolutions

During the second half of the fourteenth century the history of communal uprisings is more clearly seen in its proper historical perspective. Not only did the fiscal demands of the monarchy increase, as a consequence of political events which endangered the very existence of the Capetian dynasty, but also the Hundred Years War and consequent brigandage ruined the country; and the Black Death and the laws relating to work and wages plunged into chaos the labour force and the prices of commodities. The burgess class advanced the claim to control the royal expenses and the use to which taxes were put. Lastly, around 1381, popular uprisings broke out in Flanders, in Paris, in Germany, in Italy and even England. It was not without good reason that the great burgess Etienne Marcel, in his famous letter to the *bonnes villes* of France and Flanders of 11 July 1358, inveighed against the disreputable counsellors surrounding the king and pitied "the good citizens, the good labourers and the good merchants without whom we cannot live". Amid so many disasters and upheavals it was hardly surprising that the communes were occasionally interrupted or even abolished.

The two facts which dominated the relationship between the communes in their weakened state and the monarchy, were on the one hand the development of public taxation, and on the other hand the crisis of sentiment which, at the risk of committing an anachronism, I should like to call the crisis of patriotism. It had been called into being by the Poitiers disaster, the military short-comings of the nobility, and the *petit gouvernement* of the dauphin Charles.

It was this upsurge of anger against the nobility which caused the burgesses of Meaux to lose their communal privilege. In 1358, like burgesses in many other towns, they made common cause against the nobility by an alliance with the peasants or *Jacques*. The mayor, John Soulas, was prepared to hand the town over to them, but the count of Joigny in a surprise move occupied the marketplace of Meaux, which lay in a sheltered position in a loop of the Marne. When the Paris contingent arrived together with several hundred peasants, Soulas gave them a great welcome. They decided to launch an attack against the marketplace, but it failed. The population suffered terrible reprisals; some were slaughtered, others were taken prisoner, and their town was burned down. The inhabitants were "accused and convicted of the crime of high treason for their detestable deed", and their commune was abolished; Meaux was henceforward administered by the *prévôt* of Paris.

In other cases we can clearly perceive that the disturbances were provoked by angry reactions to material damage and the fear of poverty. The staggering increase in taxes, the birth of an inquisitorial fiscal organization, the serious repercussions affecting municipal budgets, the blow dealt to the financial independence of towns, the complicity of the *gens du roi* and the burgess oligarchies did not only harm the towns which had a commune, but in certain communes brought about the loss of this special privilege of theirs.

The free towns of the fourteenth century had two sources of income: 'patrimonial' revenues and 'extraordinary' receipts. They owned houses, which they let at quit-rent, they owned marketplaces, vices, drains, sometimes mills; in fact all kinds of sources of revenue which used to be farmed by the royal *prévôt* and had now become the property of the town, wherever the *prévôté* had been abolished. They pocketed fines, seigneurial dues on property transfers, taxes payable on entering the burgess class or joining a gild. They offered for sale municipal offices and *sergenteries*. All these sources of income put together did not cover the standing expenses, quite apart from the running costs of the fortifications. Often they did not amount to a fifth of the budget. The other four-fifths came, at Amiens for example, from annual taxes agreed to in principle by the population and varying from place to place. The nature of these taxes and the way they were levied caused endless protests. The majority of the inhabitants preferred the *taille*, a wealth tax, provided it was fairly assessed. But the upper burgess class, who ran the town's affairs, favoured indirect taxation, or *aides*, the most widespread of which was the wine tax. But whether the tax was direct or indirect, the wealthy burgesses made sure they did not pay the sum legally required of them. In one town they obtained exemption by invoking a privilege; in another, the method of assessment spared those most able to pay. It was estimated that at Amiens the 670 most wealthy inhabitants, representing a quarter of the population, did not pay as much as an eighth part of the wine tax. These taxes, before the period we are investigating in this chapter, could have been levied without the king's consent.

But in St Louis' time the officials of the *Comptes* had asked to examine municipal budgets and the custom had grown up of requesting in advance a royal ratification for the taxes. In this way it became possible to obtain letters of *octroi* or permission to raise the tax, valid for two or three years; the *octroi* was also granted to enable borrowing. The magistrates thus covered themselves against any possible reproach by the *Cour des comptes*, and against complaints from the taxpayer. The king, for his part, taking cognizance in this way of the municipal budgets, without needing to compel the burgesses to produce their accounts for him, was tempted to take a little for himself, a temptation he did not resist for very long. Moreover, as Domat observed, it was in the king's interest that towns should not ruin themselves and that he should be able to prevent them from so doing by withholding the *octroi*. The towns still retained the freedom to assess and collect taxes. But from the mid-fourteenth century, the king introduced fiscal officers called *élus*. Usually recruited locally, they closely observed the echevins, the tax-collectors and clerks, and gathered information on the details of their management of affairs, after borrowing from them methods of accountancy, or else advising them to adopt their own methods. Thus the development of the public tax kept pace with the development of urban budgets, not without prejudice to the latter's independence. As a final blow to the private pocket, calls for funds came both from the royal officers and from the municipalities; so that anger often caused the two categories of extorter to become confused in the popular mind, so that they seemed in league to oppress the poor. In fact, they did very often borrow each other's methods to that end.

Scattered through the sources, especially in legal documents, are proofs of the strength of this popular resentment. On occasion it even went so far as to aim at the complete overthrow of French society and the kingdom of France. In 1358 an agitator called Jean de la Mare was executed at Abbeville; he had boasted that he could provoke a civil war, and had declared "that he had only to lift a finger, and there would not be a single rich man or woman left in Abbeville, and that if only the mayor and seven or eight of the townspeople were dead, everyone in the town would be equal, and he would like to see all the enemies of the kingdom of France, whether English or Saracens, arrayed before the walls of Abbeville".

Amiens and Rouen have been fortunate in having learned and conscientious historians who enable us to form an exact idea of the life of these two great communes in the fourteenth century. The levying of permanent taxes to defend French soil and pay the ransom for King John, the inopportune suppression of the hearth tax by Charles V on his deathbed, followed shortly afterwards by new levies, provoked in both these towns a period of turmoil, as a result of which Rouen lost its liberties and those of Amiens were definitively curtailed. In 1358 the two communes sided with Charles the Bad. In 1381 they joined the popular movement threatening the monarchies of the Western world. Fortunately for them, the popular uprisings had ill-defined aims. In France they were independent of each other. Only the uprising at Ghent became well enough known to be taken as a model. Amiens and Rouen suffered as a result of these sporadic uprisings the usual consequences of this type of occurrence. The course of events was as follows.

At the beginning of the fourteenth century the commune of Amiens was well-organized. It had, from 1292, enjoyed perpetual possession of the royal provostship (*prévôté royale*). It had sole charge of its finances and boasted that it could defend itself, only occasionally accepting a garrison. In many towns the gilds did not participate in the management of affairs until quite late in the day; in fact, the gilds themselves are, in some towns, a phenomenon of a much later date than most historians imagine. In Amiens, however, from the earliest days of the commune, precedence was enjoyed by the dealers in woad, who made the region the main area for processing the substance, and traded in it from Amiens. They monopolized the offices of mayor, echevins and accountants and, in spite of the decline in the woad trade and the economic changes which occurred at the close of the Middle Ages, this commerce retained for a considerable time its political pre-eminence. Below these merchants, small societies of craftsmen and shop-keepers formed professional groups enjoying monopolies, and at the bottom of the scale was a seething mass of dissatisfied, unruly workmen and journeymen. Until 1382 religious confraternities of craftsmen, of the 'banners', each one with a 'mayor' at its head, took part, though in fairly small numbers, in the renewal of the *échevinage* which was recruited by a two-tier vote. There was, therefore, a 'democratic' element in the constitution of Amiens.

As early as the reign of Philip the Fair the burgesses of Amiens had shown the king that the Picards were an obstinate race. They had committed "certain offences, acts of disobedience and other crimes", which had been punished by the temporary abolition of the offices of echevin and of mayor (1307). In 1356 the wealthier burgesses of Amiens appear to have sided with the reformers. They would have remained loyal to the regent, Charles, if they had not been led astray by the trickery of the king of Navarre. He posed at first as a peacemaker and when he entered Amiens on 9 November 1357 he received an enthusiastic welcome. The outcome is well-known – the break between the dauphin and the reformers, the bloody events of 22 February 1358, and Charles' escape. The burgesses of Amiens shut their gates against him. They undertook to help Étienne Marcel, elected Charles the Bad as their leader and handed the town over to him on 16 September 1358. But the constable of Saint-Pol recaptured Amiens and put down the rebellion with great cruelty. The 'upper' burgesses in power had led the uprising, and they paid dearly. The mayor, Firmin de Coquerel, and at least a score of his accomplices were beheaded. The entire body of echevins was removed from office, and fresh elections created an unprecedented innovation by installing in municipal office a majority of men from the middle class who had never been echevins before. They proved powerless to restore order, and the regent had to take charge of the town himself for a time. He was in any case anxious to become reconciled to the burgess oligarchy, since it was on their class that the monarchy relied throughout France. Charles restored to the wealthy families of Amiens all their former privileges.

Those responsible for the high-handed introduction of the tax for the ransom of King John the Good did no more than imitate the system of municipal contributions, and paid not the least attention to the popular protests against the weight and inequality of the indirect taxes. The result at Amiens was the interference, which had been avoided hitherto, of the *gens du roi*, in the assessment and collection of the municipal taxes themselves, which became more and more onerous. The *bailli* applied the *octrois* agreed to by the king, which thereby acquired a tyrannical flavour. It even happened that the *bailli* and the royal *élus* took it upon themselves to levy the taxes granted and to bring pressure to bear on those reluctant to pay.

The news of Charles V's abolition of the hearth-tax because of belated scruples, which proved a great embarrassment to the new government, brought great rejoicing to Amiens, and the party of 'banner mayors' judged the time had come to replace the indirect taxes by a direct tax proportional to wealth, and to replace the system of imposed *octrois* by the older custom of popular consent. Accordingly, in 1381, they laid before the Paris Parlement their complaints against the municipal oligarchy. The Paris Parlement did not refuse to give its opinion. It considered itself not just as a court of justice but also as an emanation of the king's court. Though regarded by the population as the upholder of equity, it was nevertheless not in favour of these popular movements which worried the privileged classes. On 1st January 1382 it pronounced its opinion on the methods of cancelling the debts of the town of Amiens.

It advocated the levying of indirect taxes and its sole recommendation was a more equitable distribution of the wine tax. At the same time the Council of Regency, which had not succeeded in obtaining money from the Estates, caused an explosion of public indignation by the arbitrary reintroduction of the public tax of twelve *deniers* per *livre* on sales. This was the signal for riots in Paris and Rouen. Amiens was involved in elections. One of the ringleaders of the reformist party who had joined the ranks of the echevins and been appointed *grand compteur* was removed from office by the king. This provoked a violent revolt, which was swiftly repressed. The town was occupied by the military, the ringleaders were exiled or tortured, and the entire commune was reorganized (1383). The most serious change was the suppression of the 'banner mayors' who were the leaders of the lower burgess class. From now on the elections and the rendering of accounts were to take place under the chairmanship of the *bailli*, assisted by *prud'hommes* of his own choice. The theory that the *taille* could not be introduced to meet the needs of the town without preliminary consent from the king, and must be applied precisely for the purpose specified in the *lettres d'octroi*, was proclaimed as if it were a legal fact by the *procureur général* of the Paris Parlement when proceedings were instituted by the commune of Amiens against the bishop and chapter in 1401. And so in the case of Amiens the end result of these fifty years of strife was to ensure the preponderance of the upper burgess class but also their ultimate surrender of authority to the king.

The commune of Rouen was abolished for good after existing for a century, following a series of popular rebellions. Rouen was then one of the largest towns in the kingdom; about the mid-thirteenth century it had a population of 40,000 inhabitants or thereabouts, and its trade flourished. But its prosperity benefited no one but the merchant aristocracy which governed the town, and the monarch who derived money from it. The *minor populus* complained to no avail. We learn from a curt little chronicler's reference that in 1281 the mayor was assassinated. In 1292 the levy of a *maltôte* provoked a popular uprising and the mob broke into the receiver's house, throwing into the street the money already collected. An effort was made to take by storm the *Château* where the masters of the exchequer were in session, but the rebels were defeated and many were hanged, while the rest were imprisoned. Philip the Fair abolished the commune and then, two years later, sold it back to the inhabitants for the sum of 12,000 *livres parisis*. Then he demanded an *aide* of 30,000 *livres*. In order to give these presents of money to the king, for the marriage of his daughter, and to grease the palm of Enguerrand de Marigny, the town had to borrow from the Lombard bankers and levy crushing taxes which the *grossi burgenses* managed to dodge. Popular complaints were laid before the Easter session of the exchequer in 1320, and were heeded at long last. King Philip the Tall adopted a different policy from his predecessors. The commissioners of enquiry informed him that the only way to ensure the "perpetual silence" of the inhabitants was to break the stranglehold of the rich. He therefore abolished the *Établissements* of Rouen and in February 1321 he promulgated the constitution which replaced them and which introduced *prud'hommes du commun* and receivers. All that remained of the former body of magistrates was a committee of peers (reduced to thirty-six members, one-third of whom were renewed annually, according to the normal method in use for the election of peers), and a mayor (appointed as before by the king from a list of three candidates). The *gardes des paroisses*, the twelve *prud'hommes* and the peers were all involved in drawing up a list of candidates. These twelve *prud'hommes*, who were elected in the first instance by the peers, the *gardes des paroisses* and the "most notable persons of the commons of the parishes" and were then co-opted annually, advised and generally supervised the mayor. Moreover the mayor was no longer entrusted with the management of important sources of revenues; these were taken over by four receivers, two of whom were chosen from among the peers and two from the *prud'hommes*.

Rouen now enjoyed semi-democratic government. Moreover, "to remove the grounds or occasion for rancour or discord", the former peers were allowed to remain in office until their death or until they retired, with the result that the installation of the middle-class burgesses in the town hall was only gradual. The former seal representing a lion seen full face, was replaced by a seal showing a placid sheep, symbolizing the preponderance of the drapers' gild. In the reign of Charles V Rouen's economic prosperity attained fresh heights.

But the great mass of the people remained sullen and threatening. They accused the municipal authorities of continuing to embezzle funds, of being unwilling to disclose their accounts, of removing the *prud'hommes* from power and of failing to summon the common people to general assemblies. In 1345 the king was obliged to take over the running of Rouen for a time and to institute an enquiry, which proved unfavourable to popular demands. In 1358 disturbances flared up again: for a time the inhabitants of Rouen espoused the cause of Charles the Bad. Finally, during the turbulent years 1381–1382, there occurred the crisis which sealed the fate of the Rouen commune. Some hundreds of cloth-workers revolted on 24 February 1382, yelling that they would not pay the tax. However, the only damage they inflicted was to pillage a few rich men's houses, and there were only two victims. On 25 February pressure was brought on the abbey of Saint-Ouen to produce a charter renouncing its legal rights over Rouen and its suburb, which leads one to think that the middle burgess class had joined the movement. On 26 February an assembly was held in which the inhabitants of Rouen swore to maintain the *Charte aux Normands*. Then the mood of exhilaration abated. The inhabitants begged the king's pardon. Very few of them were executed, but the commune was abolished.

Money was needed at this time to finance the Flanders expedition. On 1 August, when an attempt was made in Rouen to collect the taxes voted by the Estates of Normandy in June, the inhabitants of Rouen drove the tax-collectors out of town, and this fresh riot went on for a few days. When Charles VI returned to France after his victory at Roosebeke, he sent commissioners to Rouen with an escort of soldiers. This time municipal liberties were confiscated for good. The king reserved the right, for himself and his successors, to "the jurisdiction, corporate body, and commune, which the mayors and peers of the town used to have". This marked the end of the Rouen commune.

The character of the insufficiently documented armed seditions which broke out in Arras in 1355 and Saint-Quentin in 1380 may be roughly surmised from the dates when they occurred. They are of the same type as the ones we have just been considering. The bloody revolt at Arras is succinctly recounted in the letters of pardon granted to the inhabitants by the king's lieutenant in Artois. Two echevins and fifteen others had been murdered in an echevin's house and their bodies thrown out of the windows; the slaughter had continued for some days. Fourteen of the culprits were executed. At Saint-Quentin, as we have seen, the town had been harshly treated by John the Good and ruined by war. The communal administration was in a state of neglect and the artisan class blamed the administration for the prevailing poverty. In 1380 there was an "uprising of the humbler folk of the town against the important and respectable people of the same". This rebellion cost the town a fine of 2,000 gold francs. In the years that followed we can see the communal assembly, apparently unable to reach a decision, constantly seeking the advice of the *bailli* and, although the commune continued to exist, its mainspring was broken.

However, it must be said that despite the external and internal troubles which undermined the communes and indeed overthrew some of them, the fourteenth century was not the century which marked their decline, and proofs of their relative vitality are often encountered in the *Recueil des ordonnances*, which do not of course cover all examples. During the fourteenth century the kings and their counsellors did not show persistent hostility towards the communes: Philip VI and Charles V seem to have acted in the spirit of St Louis, who had a respect for traditions and unalienable rights, joined with a loathing of disorder and confusion. Occasionally, the commune was protected against the encroachments of the royal officers. The *Recueil des ordonnances* contains instances of this, which are certainly not exhaustive, in the case of Niort, Abbeville, Mantes, Saint-Quentin itself, etc. Even though letters of confirmation of commune or of royal protection, or of perpetual union with the royal domain, or of noble rank conferred upon magistrates, were a source of profit to the royal treasury, they are nevertheless proof of goodwill on the part of the monarch. For this reason it is impossible to entertain the view that the monarchy sought to put an end to the communes.

4. Communes which revived in the fourteenth century

That is not the whole story. The fourteenth century saw the birth of one or two new communes, or perhaps it would be more accurate to say the revival of communes which had long been dead.

In the twelfth century Saintes had possessed a commune, confirmed by Eleanor of Aquitaine in 1199, and provided with the customs of La Rochelle. Nothing was heard of it in the thirteenth century: probably the rather idle burgesses of the town had not troubled to keep it going. In 1347 they asked Philip VI to grant them a commune. After mature deliberation "in full council", and in view of the loyalty of the inhabitants and the damage and expense they had suffered in the wars, he granted them as a special favour and free of charge the possibility of having from that time corporate body, community, and 'university' with the liberties enjoyed by the inhabitants of La Rochelle, and the right to elect a mayor as often as they wished.

In 1215 Cognac had also possessed a commune granted by John Lackland and enjoying the customs of Niort and Saint-Jean-d'Angély; there too the inhabitants had allowed their rights to lapse. When Charles of Spain, constable of France, received the county of Angoulême from the king he thought it necessary for the inhabitants to be able to hold meetings; for this they needed a common meeting place, a common purse, a bell to summon the inhabitants to meetings, a legal system, a mayor, councillors and elected echevins. And so he granted them, in May 1352, a "sworn commune", *communitatem juratam*, with institutions partly modelled on the *Établissements* of Rouen. He stipulated that if the mayor and his townspeople helped any of his enemies, the commune would be abolished. Like the other thirteenth-century communes, Cognac seems to have been required to play a military role.

The commune of Angoulême which was also founded by John Lackland, with the customs of Rouen, in 1203, had quickly disappeared. The town was annexed by the English according to the terms of the treaty of Brétigny and had become the Black Prince's favourite residence. It surrendered to the French in 1372. In letters of January and March 1373, which are of great interest, Charles V re-established the commune, without concealing the fact that he thereby intended to make it a fortress for himself capable, because of the unity of its inhabitants and the extent of their franchises, of holding out against the enemy. He wished the burgesses of Angoulême to be better able to defend and keep in their entirety their own rights; this is almost the same formula as the one in the charters of military commune granted to the towns of Poitou by Eleanor and John Lackland. Charles V did not regard the inhabitants as having renounced their fealty to him after the town was annexed by the king of England: "They acknowledged us publicly as their natural and superior lord." And so he granted them a sworn commune, similar in every respect to the one enjoyed by Saint-Jean-d'Angély, with the same customs of town and suburb, franchises, privileges and statutes constituting its force and effect, and he commanded his officers to place no obstacle in its way. The nobles owning property in Angoulême and for two leagues around were to help the town to defend itself: they were to contribute to the cost of the watch and the fortifications. Following the system of the *Établissements* of Rouen there were to be 100 peers, which would include a mayor, twelve echevins, twelve councillors and a sub-mayor. The rules for the election of a mayor embodied Charles V's favourite ideas; the 100 peers elected the mayor according to one of these three methods: either the election was to take place with the help of the Holy Spirit, through the inspiration of one of the 100 peers who would present three names for the royal seneschal to choose from; or the peers would proceed 'by scrutiny' and also put up three names; or else, thirdly, a compromise method would be followed according to certain specified rules. The peers would meet every month and would keep minutes of their discussions. The rest of the charter concerns trade, the hire of farm-workers and public hygiene.

Poitou was not the only region of France which saw the resurrection of a commune during the first part of the Hundred Years War. Saint-Valéry-sur-Somme, as we have seen, was deprived of its commune in 1234. In August 1376 John of Artois, count of Eu and lord of Saint-Valéry, yielded to the requests of the inhabitants who, without breathing a word of their relations with the monks, pleaded the disappearance of their charters, which had been destroyed during the wars by the king's enemies. He declared that he was aware of their loyal services which he hoped they would continue to give him, and granted them law and commune according to the usages and customs of Saint-Quentin with echevins, a bell, a large and small pillory, a seal and a suburb. In actual fact the charter owed nothing to the Saint-Quentin charter, but it was liberal, and it effected a judicious distribution of authority and advantages between the magistrates and the lord. The mayor was to be chosen by the lord from two candidates put forward by the mayor in office and the echevins, with the consent of the commune. The mayor could receive into the commune anyone he wished, but the outsider whom he welcomed must, before a year had elapsed, swear the communal oath, or he would receive no help from it. Those whose houses had been demolished were expected to rebuild them. Jurisdiction was equitably shared out, together with its advantages, between the lord and the commune; only the lord might take cognizance of cases of 'high' justice, but the mayor and echevins took part in passing sentence and, in trials concerning freemen of the lord, who were not members of the commune, the mayor and echevins were to come and see and hear how justice was done. Finally the members of the commune owed military service and *chevauchée* at their own expense, and were obliged to find ways of housing the lord's knights when they came to town on business or to wage wars.

There was a visible effort on both sides to forestall disagreements and to respect the rights of everyone involved, and the lord evidently intended to have at Saint-Valéry devoted subjects who would help him vanquish his enemies. Future events were to prove the wisdom of these aims, for Saint-Valéry had to resist numerous attacks. But, in 1376, the monks protested because they had not been consulted; an agreement concluded in 1383 with the lord of Saint-Valéry mollified them, though it merely touched on one or two points of detail. The decree of 1376 was confirmed in 1488 by John of Brabant, lord of the town; a few new provisions did not change the conciliatory tone of the charter, which was the work of intelligent, practical-minded men. The burgesses of this little town which had suffered such battering and been exposed to such threats had managed to interest the lord in their cause and to shake off the tutelage of the Church.

An episode from the history of Saint-Maixent proves that, in the time of John the Good, legists applied only to the communes the protective fiction of corporate 'body and college'. The communes were still regarded as privileged entities whose behaviour deserved a certain indulgence, rather like noblemen who could draw their sword without causing offence. There was no question of allowing towns without a commune to usurp similar rights. Saint-Maixent was at this time a town of moderate size; in 1947 it had 4,800 inhabitants; it was probably the same size or even larger, in the fourteenth century, since the gates of the town are still where they were, and in the eighteenth century it was listed as one of the centres with over 4,500 inhabitants. The administration and the maintenance of law and order were shared between the royal *prévôt* and the *prévôt* of the famous abbey, whose role was gradually declining in importance. One or two petty lords of an aggressive turn of mind had fortresses giving on to the street, in particular Savary de Vivonne, lord of the Tour-Chabot, whose men were constantly engaged in plunder. On 26 June 1352, when a fair was in progress, Savary's *pedites seu brigandi* seized two burgesses and attempted to hold one of them in the Chabot tower until he had paid a ransom. They began to stone the burgesses, shouting the seditious cry of Gascony!, which was one of the English rallying cries. Saint-Maixent possessed a bell with which to give warning of fires or the approach of the enemy. The burgesses rang this bell, gathered together and, with the help of some outsiders who had come to the fair, set fire to the tower gate, compelled the aggressors to surrender and handed them over to the captain of the town's militia, who placed them under guard.

Savary de Vivonne had the audacity to institute proceedings against the inhabitants, and the king's proctor at his instigation accused them before the seneschal of Poitou. He maintained that the burgesses had incurred great guilt, not only because of the fire, but because, without the status of *corps et communauté*, they had rung the bell, taken up arms, formed a conspiracy and a confederation, and had pooled their resources to pay the expenses of the case they brought against Savary. The mayor and a certain number of notables, together with one or two belligerent monks who had joined their ranks, went to prison. But the king, taking into consideration the excesses committed by Savary's followers and the damage suffered by the town during the recent wars – it had been burned down by the duke of Lancaster – granted letters of pardon and ordered the inhabitants who had been arrested to be set free. They had come very close to being condemned for defending themselves at a time when they did not form a corporate body and college, for it was alleged that they should have asked the king to exercise the kind of repressive measures which a commune was able to wield independently by virtue of the rights of burgess association which it enjoyed.

5. Conclusion

In conclusion it must be said that although the communal institution became insecure during the fourteenth century, it still remained intact. We have seen that although the commune, on the eve of the Hundred Years War, was discredited by the very people who benefited from it, was undermined by the blows dealt it by the king's officers, and although in certain famous cases it dealt its own death-blow, these examples of suicide in the fourteenth century were not on the whole very numerous. We are not in a position to affirm that the majority of the communes extended their life beyond this date, but there are many cases of communes which did, and not merely in an attenuated form. The re-establishment of communes which had been suspended, the revival of communes which had long since disappeared, together with the attempt of the inhabitants of Saint-Maixent to form an association, which the *procureurs du roi* stigmatized as illegal because they had no communal charter, are highly significant events. The fact that there was a desire at Saintes, at Cognac, at Angoulême, at Saint-Valéry and possibly elsewhere, to revive the military pattern which grew up in the time of Philip Augustus and Eleanor of Aquitaine, is proof of the confidence felt by certain princes in the effectiveness of the sworn association in the defence of the country. The convenience of a system which left to the burgesses the responsibility of urban administration, while extracting from them a considerable annual tax in return for the concession of a commune, became most apparent when the concession was withdrawn: the utter confusion into which the town was often plunged with the change of regime gave both lords and burgesses food for thought. Lastly the aversion felt by the French to destroying established institutions, their respect for custom and a variety of usages, go far towards explaining why the communes survived: it is hardly surprising that it was only the total upheaval of the Revolution which caused their final destruction.

CHAPTER 4

The French communes at the end of the Middle Ages

1. General characteristics

During the disastrous years when the English, the Burgundians and the Armagnacs were tramping across France, we must not expect to find many traces of a distinct communal existence, or of a rise and fall materially different from the advances or setbacks which marked the history of towns with simple franchises. The burgesses, no matter where they lived, maintained as best they could the partial security which the country-dwellers envied so much; legal titles therefore counted for very little. The main need was to possess an active municipality which made the best possible use of its meagre resources, and was able to defend itself against the demands of princes and the depredations of robber bands. The magistrates in these towns acquired by sheer force of circumstance an independence seldom enjoyed by the magistrates of the earlier communes; whether or not their archives contained a communal charter had scarcely any bearing on their daily life.

The idea of a town with an *échevinage* now acquired greater significance than that of the sworn commune. The concept of *corps et collège* became less narrow and rigid. It was less jealously kept within its former limits by the jurists: many *échevinages* behaved as if they did legally constitute a *corps et collège*. On the other hand it would seem that in the vocabulary of the royal chancery (as is already evident in Charles V's mandates and letters) all communes clearly recognized as such were referred to simply as "good towns". A reply given by Charles VI to the inhabitants of Noyon in 1414 is rather striking. The mayor and *jurés*, he said, have explained to us "that they constitute a corporate body and commune, and therefore have a belfry, a bell, a seal and everything duly appertaining to a corporate body and commune, . . . and on these grounds the said mayor and *jurés* have the oversight and cognizance of the government and public order in the said town". The king complied with a request they made to him, but made no reference to the communal privileges; he declared that he wished "always to provide for the good government and public order of the good towns" of his kingdom. Documents relating to certain communes which continued to be organized exactly as they had been before, Eu for example, have, even in the fourteenth century, dropped the term 'commune'. Such texts can of course be matched by others showing the opposite tendency. The monarchy was still so threatened that, in theory, it seemed essential to hold institutions like the communes in high regard. We shall see how in the mid-fifteenth century a reward bestowed on loyal burgesses took the form of a charter granting a commune; although this was an isolated event, it must not be overlooked.

In the fourteenth century communes frequently disappeared, either because they destroyed themselves or were banned by their lord. This is not true of the fifteenth century. When catalogues are available for the entire geographical area covered in this volume, such as already exist for Artois, Poitou and Berry, I feel certain we shall find very few exceptions to the hypothesis I am now putting forward. One such exception is Arras, which was brutally stripped of its commune and its liberties by Louis XI in 1479; even then the new inhabitants who settled in the town, now known as 'Franchise', possessed ancient liberties. In 1440 the inhabitants of Beaune, an unruly, intractable mob, refused to allow the governor of Burgundy's men to enter the town; Duke Philip the Good deprived them of their commune and their liberties, but restored both shortly afterwards. To sum up: under the direct line of Valois kings, the communes continued to exist, but their history splits into two quite distinct parts, namely the first half of the fifteenth century and the reign of Louis XI.

2. The communes in the reign of Charles VII

During the English occupation the history of the communes, as I have just stated, merges with the history of "good towns" in general. Concerning the miseries suffered by the towns and their utter determination to continue in existence all these annals tell the same story. Beauvais, Amiens, Tournai, Bayonne, all communes, were ruined as were the towns which formerly possessed a commune, such as Compiègne, Laon and Sens, and the free towns of Auxerre and Tours. In all these towns the burgesses behaved with a combination of discretion and courage. They became, in spite of themselves, warriors and diplomats, and functioned, whether they wished to or not, as defenders of the monarchy and of national unity. The English invasions, the acts of plunder committed by the *Écorcheurs*, restored to them the habits of spontaneous activity, a spirit of initiative and self-denial which they had lost. Charles VII, the 'king of Bourges', who went on to conquer his own kingdom of France, asked enormous sacrifices of the towns, not only in the form of taxes agreed by assemblies of Estates, but in the form of direct demands. He begged or demanded of them sums of money, men, experienced crossbowmen or gunners, weapons of war, munitions, and carts; but for their help he would probably not have taken the fortress of Montereau in 1437, nor that of Pontoise in 1441. There were frequent general assemblies of the inhabitants to discuss the requests received and to appoint delegates to call upon the king or the war leaders. They were often obliged to cope with imminent dangers. Since the towns were thrown back on their own resources they had to take weighty decisions, and discussions often took place in circumstances of danger or anxiety. They corresponded with each other, kept each other informed of what was going on, and took concerted action. In 1432 the mayor of the commune of Beauvais had an interview at Senlis with the attorneys of Senlis, Compiègne and other good towns of the region to discuss a return to work during the truce. Later on, miniature campaigns were organized against the *Écorcheurs*. The main concern of the town was to avoid looting, and the king's soldiery were distrusted almost as much as the gangs of *Écorcheurs* or the English. Towns which had no fortifications built them, and the magistrates had the gates closed the moment a warning was given by the look-outs. Sometimes the royal troops were prevented from passing through the town and refused provisions, or else they were obliged to pass through in small groups, closely escorted by an armed guard of suspicious burgesses. When Charles VII entered Troyes in 1429 he concluded a genuine treaty with the inhabitants in which he promised in particular not to impose a garrison upon them.

The impression conveyed by the documents is the same, whether they relate to communes or free towns, or even towns without privileges in which mortmain still persisted. Charles VII, especially at the beginning of his reign, was obliged to assume without proof they would help him; after his ultimate victory enabled him to impose his wishes, he did not long bear a grudge against those towns which patiently endured or supported from choice an English or Burgundian garrison. Bayonne, for example, which Dunois had to retake by storm, had its franchises curtailed, but was not under a cloud for long, and both sides showed much good will. Towns which had proved loyal were heaped with favours. Charles VII confirmed their privileges and even absorbed some of them into the royal domain, a step which was greatly appreciated. Occasionally he granted exemptions from taxes or garrison duty, or he gave gifts of money, to relieve a population reduced to penury. Of particular interest to us is the fact that he once actually granted a commune charter as a reward.

No single event in his reign was more painful to Charles VII than the revolt of the Praguerie "under the protection of his son". It was on this occasion that the town of Saint-Maixent demonstrated its affection for him. The rebel duke of Alençon was occupying Niort and hoped to seize Saint-Maixent before marching on Poitiers, where he planned to take the king by surprise. An act of treason surrendered the castle of Saint-Maixent to him on 3 April 1440. The inhabitants of Niort, who were close behind the soldiers, entered the houses, removed the furniture and objects of value, and began transporting them to Niort. But on the orders of an intrepid abbot, the abbey of Saint-Maixent refused to submit, and so did the Porte de la Croix district of the town. A former mercenary soldier called Pierre Doulx who had been a plunderer in his youth but had retired to Saint-Maixent, leapt on to a horse and rode without stopping to Poitiers to raise the alarm. Pierre de Brézé and Richemont left at once with a force of 400 lances, followed some hours later by the king himself. They occupied the town. The duke of Alençon fled and the garrison capitulated. Niort was punished by the loss of its commune rights, which were not restored for two years, and by the loss of its status as the seat of the *élus sur le fait des aides pour la guerre*, which was transferred to Saint-Maixent. Pierre Doulx was awarded a pension, and the town of Saint-Maixent received a communal charter, together with a set of magnificent armorial bearings. The "serfs and the inhabitants ... in gratitude and as an eternal reminder of their great and good loyalty and valour", and also on the recommendation of several princes of the blood and of the Great Council, were to have "corporate body, college and town community" and the power to "choose each year, to govern the said town, two of their number, who thus elected would have the keys of the gates, and the custody and government of the same town, with the compulsion, cognizance, dues and profits" appertaining thereto; the receivers were to render their accounts to them and to restore to them what remained in the town's coffers.

This charter of April 1440 specified nothing more. The inhabitants of Saint-Maixent were left free to choose, in agreement with the monarchy, the system of government most appropriate to a town with a corporate body and a college. The word 'commune' was not mentioned, but I have no hesitation in regarding this charter as a commune charter and not merely a simple institution of *échevinage*. The "Statutes and ordinances of the house and *échevinage* of the town and community of Saint-Maixent drawn up by the mayor and echevins of the same, in accordance with the privileges given to them by our lord the king and his predecessors, concerning the administration, public order, government and affairs of the said town", which were published in a general assembly on 14 April 1506, together with various documents subsequent to the 1440 charter, do indeed make it clear that not only did the two elected representatives give way to a mayor who governed with the help of echevins (which was true of many towns which were not communes), but also that Saint-Maixent had all the attributes of a commune: the qualifying circumstance of a corporate body, and a college, a seal, a common meeting house and a belfry. The documents make no reference now to the oath of mutual aid uniting the inhabitants, because this ancient formula, which had formerly contained an essential truth, was outdated for reasons which have been set out earlier in this book. For the same reason we should not be surprised to see the term 'commune' replaced by the 'community'.

If we examine the letters of September 1451 with which Charles VII regulated the form of the elections of magistrates at Montreuil-sur-Mer, an old commune dating from 1188, we perceive that he has regard for "the former privileges of the foundation and creation of the law and *commune* of this town", and that he had listened to the plea of his "good friends the mayor, echevins, burgesses, inhabitants and *community*" of his town of Montreuil-sur-Mer. The second term is the modern one, and the other is only used from force of habit. In any case the two terms *communia* and *communitas* had been interchangeable for a very long time.

However, let us return to the Saint-Maixent charter. It is most important to realize that it was the king's intention to honour a body of burgesses who had, at a very critical juncture, safeguarded his person. Consequently he made sure that in all its external signs it ranked with those towns he particularly cherished, such as Tournai. In 1426 Tournai had received from Charles VII the privilege of adding the royal escutcheon in the chief of its coat-of-arms, and the franchises it enjoyed as an ancient commune were respected and defended by the Great Council against the officers of the Crown. Similarly Charles VII allowed the inhabitants of Saint-Maixent to carry as their coat of arms "a shield with a gold crown on a field of gules and three gold fleurs-de-lis in chief". He also allowed them to form a commune on the same footing as the famous *communiae regis* of the thirteenth century and the towns which the Parlement had recognized as enjoying the rights of 'corporate body and college'.

The case of Saint-Maixent is interesting on another count, besides being a late example of the granting of a commune. It shows just how much the royal counsellors were prepared to concede in the fifteenth century when granting a town a mark of royal favour – very little in fact. The mayor of Saint-Maixent (when it had one) had no legal rights, but was merely empowered to impose one or two trifling fines when he went the round of the market-halls and discovered an instance of fraud or infringement of the regulations. The burgesses as a whole were at liberty to admire the gold escutcheon and the three gold fleurs-de-lis on their armorial bearings, but that was more or less the sum total of what they had gained. The opening article of the 1506 statutes is couched in terms which historians of Saint-Maixent would have done well to notice. "And first there shall be in the said corporate body, college and community no more than thirty persons, who shall be known as echevins." This corporate body and college is indeed now nothing more than the town corporation. It is true that the mayor of Saint-Maixent, according to Article 12, "shall call a general assembly of inhabitants by ringing the bell to discuss the community's business, at least four times a year". As early as 1441 the two elected representatives instituted by royal charter called a meeting to introduce a duty on wine to help repair the fortifications. There was, as I have already indicated, a revival of general assemblies in the fifteenth century, which is explicable by the fact that the municipal magistrates had not had to take such weighty decisions for a very long time. But this must not lead us to assume that the government of communes and *bonnes villes* became 'democratic' overnight. For example, the report of the general assembly held at Saint-Maixent in 1441 informs us that there were fifty people present, "those who claimed to be the larger and sounder part of the burgesses, merchants and inhabitants of this town".

Unfortunately, our information on this fascinating question is scanty; it certainly does not suggest that the lesser burgess class in France attempted to participate effectively in the deliberations of the general assemblies. Before war broke out again in 1415 the citizens were most reluctant to leave their work to attend such gatherings. In Noyon, in 1414, the mayor and *jurés* complained that the members of the commune were "unwilling to go into the *chambre* of the said town when they were summoned there to discuss and consider matters affecting government and public order". One wonders whether, during the war, the majority of the inhabitants showed any great eagerness to know what was going on and what expenses the town had to bear. Flammermont supplies some most interesting facts about Senlis, which enable us to form a reasonably accurate picture of what went on in most other towns. The attorneys who had governed Senlis since the suppression of the commune summoned the general assembly whenever circumstances required it or a group of citizens requested it, because it seemed a good plan "to forestall the grumbles of the common people". There were sometimes as many as 400 persons present. But when the notables took the trouble to attend, only a small quorum was thought necessary for decision-making; sometimes no more than fifteen people came, although absence was punishable by a fine. The assembly was held in the *grande salle* of the town hall, with the bailiff's lieutenant in the chair; near the desk at which were seated the royal officials and the attorneys, sat the notables; at the back of the room were the common people, who listened in silence to the town councillors and the chairman. The vote was taken by acclaim without any detailed discussion. During the meeting of 26 December 1446 a certain Jean Oudot wished "to point out something for the good and the advantage of the town". The royal proctor invited him go stand on a chair so he could be heard more clearly, but Jean Oudot, "utterly dismayed, could not utter a word", and withdrew. On the other hand, when it was decided to abide by the decision of a small council instead of the general assembly, the burgesses took umbrage and flocked to the town hall. Human nature never changes.

3. Louis XI and the communes

Charles VII does not seem to have intervened often in the internal affairs of towns. It was enough for his purpose to extract money and men from the burgess class. The royal officials continued their policy of encroachment, and the never-ending legal battles went on, but little effort was made to modify the institutions which governed the communes or the free towns. Charles VII, despite the forced effusiveness of his letters to his "dearly beloved" inhabitants of Tournai, Amiens, Rheims and other 'good towns', felt no personal interest whatsoever either for the middle classes or for the humble folk, a fact which probably explains the indifference he showed to Joan of Arc and Jacques Coeur. He was a nobleman's king. Contemporaries noted that delegates sent from towns found it difficult to gain admittance to him.

Louis XI was totally different; we must now examine the attitude adopted towards the communes by this monarch who was a friend of the burgess class. He felt no sympathy for what he called the "simple folk" – craftsmen, small shopkeepers or peasants. He put down every popular uprising in his reign with barbarous cruelty. The subjects he understood best, and among whose number he found loyal, devoted friends whom he could call on for money, were wealthy burgesses, able to understand his policy and with an interest in supporting it. Needless to say, he would have crushed any revolutionary commune, any sworn association whose members had promised each other mutual aid in order to obstruct his designs. Had he known the history of Saint-Quentin in the twelfth century he would have shrugged his shoulders with rage. But he avoided, on principle, quarrelling with those communes still in existence, because he counted on taking advantage of their form of government.

He had also, no doubt, learned wisdom from his uncle Duke Philip the Good, who thought it advisable to treat his Burgundian communes with respect. During the period when Louis had taken refuge with Duke Philip, two major lawsuits took place in which communes were involved. In 1455 the town of Dijon had instituted criminal proceedings, which dragged on for years, against a great lord who enjoyed considerable credit at court, Jean de Bauffremont. He was guilty of violating communal rights in the matter of arrest: he had dragged a swindler out of the Jacobin monastery where he had sought asylum. The duke, who exacted large sums of money from the inhabitants of Dijon, upheld their rights and obliged de Bauffremont to go to prison. In 1458 the inhabitants of Beaune, whose liberties he had once confiscated but very soon restored, were accused by the duke's officers of disposing of public land in such a way as to reduce the tax they were required to pay. Proceedings were instituted, as a result of which Philip the Good obliged the commune to modify the incidence of the tax, which was not bringing him in enough money, but on the other counts he declared in favour of the inhabitants. These two incidents gave the dauphin Louis food for thought. He subsequently adopted the practice of exacting a great deal of money from the burgesses in charge of a town, while at the same time protecting them against the nobility and if necessary against the royal officials.

Historians make no reference to Louis XI's policy towards the communes, but he certainly had a policy, which at first sight appears surprisingly lenient. He was daunted neither by the word 'commune' nor the idea it embodied. On his accession in August 1461 he confirmed the privileges of the town of Tournai. In November 1461 he confirmed the privileges guaranteed by his predecessors "to the mayor, echevins, consuls, peers and community of La Rochelle" and uttered the words "community and college". He even increased the town's franchises and reduced its taxes but, after trying to change the mayoralty into a royal office for the benefit of one of his loyal supporters, he renounced arbitrary measures of this kind. In 1472, after the death of his brother Charles of France and the restoration of La Rochelle to the royal domain, Louis XI, before entering the town, swore on bended knee, his hands clasped by the mayor's, to respect its franchises. On the same day of November 1461 he had received a petition from the "corporate body, college and community" of Niort, and had ennobled the mayor, the echevins and the sworn councillors. The following year he received the humble plea of "his beloved mayor, *jurés*, burgesses, commoners and inhabitants of his town and commune of Saint-Jean-d'Angély", and, in view of their loyalty during the war against the English, he confirmed the liberties which Charles V had granted them. Then he turned his attention to the communes which had only recently returned to French rule: at the request of his dearly beloved mayor, jurats and commune of his town and city of Bordeaux, he cancelled the right which Charles VII had kept, of appointing five of the jurats, thus conserving the municipal jurisdiction. At the same time he confirmed the privileges of Bourg-en-Guyenne. In July 1462 he confirmed the customs of the "inhabitants and commune" of Aigueperse, who had "a corporate body, a counsulship, an *arche*, a seal and a communal house". After his brother's death he became reconciled with the burgesses of Saintes, whom he had formerly treated as enemies, and confirmed their privileges. In 1477 he pardoned the inhabitants of Arras for their former resistance and confirmed the privileges of "the said clergy, nobles, mayor, echevins, corporate body and community, burgesses, commoners and inhabitants of the said town". In 1478 he confirmed the privileges of the "town and commune" of Beaune.

However, I must repeat what I said when discussing Saint-Maixent: in the documents of Louis XI's reign, what constituted the 'corporate body and college', as far as the king and his chancery were concerned, was not the sum total of the inhabitants, but the corporate body of the town (*corps de ville*). Niort, for example, had a "corporate body and college and community numbering one hundred persons, namely the mayor, twelve echevins, and twelve sworn councillors and seventy-five peers". In 1475 Louis XI declared that Angers had been impoverished by its bad government, for lack of a 'community', and he decided that it should have "a corporate body and a community", consisting of a mayor, eighteen echevins and thirty-six councillors, a *procureur* and a clerk": the "community" was reduced to fifty-seven people. We have seen above that, when the town of Franchise, which replaced Arras, received privileges in 1481, the king wished to "have a corporate body and community, consisting of twelve echevins, a clerk or *greffier* and a *procureur*". Thus the term 'commune' meant something different to him from what it meant to a king like Philip Augustus or to modern historians, and it would be easy to point to contradictions and inconsistencies in his use of the word. The commune or community was an oligarchy, at times even a tiny oligarchy, governing a town which may not have originally possessed a sworn association of burgesses.

We encounter this idea again in the seemingly liberal constitutions granted by Louis XI to certain 'good towns', of which Tours is the most famous example. Like several other towns on the banks of the Loire this place had, ever since the reign of John the Good, been governed by elected representatives or *élus*; originally they had been chosen by the general assembly of the inhabitants to look after the fortifications, and they had gradually extended their mandate. Judicial power was still in the hands of royal officials, and there were no complaints at the way the *élus* were administering affairs. Impelled by his mania for change, and "wishing to augment and increase the honours and prerogatives of our town and city as he has done elsewhere, and to inspire the inhabitants of the town with the courage and desire to govern it even better", Louis XI decided that Tours should have a mayor and twenty-four echevins, and that the echevins should have "the same power, justice, prerogatives and pre-eminences" as the magistrates of La Rochelle. Louis wanted Tours to become a municipality, with prerogatives and honours heaped upon it, so that it would be at his mercy and could refuse him nothing. And indeed Tours was from that time obliged to suffer all the king's caprices and pay crushing taxes.

The word 'commune' was not mentioned in Louis XI's letters to Tours. He did, it is true, attempt to exert control over the *échevinage* by according wide powers to the general assembly of inhabitants. But, in Louis XI's day as in Charles VII's, this was pure pretence. What Louis XI really thought about general assemblies is expressed in his letters for Franchise: "All general assemblies of large communities are at times potentially dangerous, and some ill-intentioned persons may, from extreme malice, lead simple folk astray." The magistrates of Franchise were forbidden to convene assemblies without the permission of the king's lieutenant.

As in the charter granted by Charles VII to Saint-Maixent, we find the expression "corporate body, college and community" in the letters obtained in 1472 by the burgesses of Fontenay-le-Comte. But the collected documents published by Guérin show clearly that Louis XI had never intended to show this small town special favour or to grant it a commune of the older type. The inhabitants of Fontenay had previously invoked the great age of their town and their castle, their ramparts and moats, their situation "quite near the sea", their cloth industry, their trade (which was not particularly famous), and the fertility of the fair land of Poitou; lastly they had referred in vague terms to their "services," and had asked for a mayor with sixty echevins and councillors, which was a large number for a town like Fontenay-le-Comte. The wealthy burgesses expressed the unanimous wish to share the *échevinage* and its advantages between them. Louis XI had promised to comply with all these requests but had done nothing at all. And so the inhabitants held an assembly and modified their claims. All they now wanted was a "permanent corporate body, college and community of no more than thirty people". The king met this request and conferred personal privileges on the thirty echevins and the mayor, known as the *élu*, but these people enjoyed very restricted functions. In any case, when Louis XI's letters were presented to the *Chambre des Comptes* and the *Trésoriers généraux des finances*, the two courts refused to ratify them. Although the king was perfectly capable of breaking down such resistance very swiftly, he did not press the point. The people of Fontenay did not obtain the ratification of his letters for many years, and then only after a case in the Paris Parlement. These events illustrate the disappointment so often felt by people to whom Louis XI had thoughtlessly made promises. They also exemplify the attention he paid to the advice given by his counsellors when it was not at too great variance with his own views. It is, moreover, quite possible that the king himself enjoined the two courts to oppose the wishes of the inhabitants of Fontenay. He was perfectly capable of such disingenuous behaviour.

By the end of Louis XI's reign the town whose archives contained ancient communal charters (*chartes de commune*) still preserved them as valid entitlements, and many so-called privileges of 'corporate body and community' had been granted to various 'good towns'. But on the whole the French towns had been brought under subjection.

What powers and what prestige did the burgess oligarchy governing these towns really possess? Very little: the only course was to obey, serve, and endure without protest Louis XI's tyranny. Henri Sée brought together the proofs of this tyranny in his book *Louis XI et les villes*, published in 1891. He cites sudden and unjustified changes in a municipal constitution, violation of privileges, the obligation to accept royal creatures in the office of mayor or echevin, or even in the humblest of positions, financial exactions which ruined towns already weighed down with debt, an order to accept a garrison, that is to say a troop of undisciplined looters, police surveillance and the obligation to turn informer, and even meddling in the activities of the confraternities. The documents subsequently published, and the publication of Louis XI's letters, have merely served to add further details to the proofs of this shameless favouritism, this petty, meddlesome despotism.

Here are a few instances. Several letters dated 1466 have survived, which Louis XI sent to the *corps municipal* of Poitiers. They have a common flavour. On 16 April the king requests the mayor, the echevins, and the Hundred of Poitiers to give the next echevin's office to fall vacant to his valet Pierre Laigneau, because he had married a Poitiers girl and wanted to live there "provided for with honour and prerogative". On 29 June he bids them send some of their number to call on him; they had been "to see our fair uncle the count of Maine to discuss various matters, of which you told me nothing". He wants to know what was going on. Such requests are normal practice in all regimes which dispense advice or use police surveillance. But the town of Poitiers had the liberty of electing its own mayor. Even so, the king ends his letters of 29 June with these words: "And in addition, let me know the name of the man you intend to elect as mayor for the current year", and do nothing "until we have informed you of our wishes in this matter . . .." On 30 July the Great Council let it be known that the king desired the outgoing mayor, Jamet Gervain, "to continue as mayor for the current year". But on 8 October, when the king heard that Maître Andrew de Conzay, the son of his beloved Hugh de Conzay, had been elected, he allowed him to hold and wield the office of mayor; "for such is our pleasure". On 15 October he changed his mind and wrote to the councillors and echevins, "If the said Conzay has obtained any letters from us, it was by pure inadvertence . . .. We desire and command you quite expressly, immediately you have read those letters, to take the keys of our said town away from the said de Conzay, and to give them to the man who was mayor last year, whom you are to obey and cause to be obeyed as your mayor . . . . For such is our pleasure, and if you do otherwise we shall be displeased with you". The following year, on 18 June, he indicated to the inhabitants the man they must elect: the echevin Colas Mouraut, whose "sense, loyalty, integrity and diligence" he appreciated. He continued: "Please act in such a way as always to give us reason to be satisfied with you."

The man chosen by the king was not always inclined to accept the office of mayor. Maître John Ducaurel, whose name was suggested to the echevins of Amiens in 1471, tried to refuse on the grounds that he was lieutenant to the *bailli* and an *élu*, and had a great deal on his hands. But Monseigneur the Grand-Maître Antoine de Chabannes, who was president at Amiens, told him "that, since it was the king's pleasure, he could not refuse". There was much discussion, "but in the end the said Maître John said that he would not dare to disobey the king's pleasure". In 1476, at Abbeville, not only the mayor but the entire body of town councillors was chosen and appointed by Louis XI. "So as to remove all disputes and ill-feeling which might arise amongst you as you drew up your new law, we have done it for you this year", he wrote, and sent them the list. He added cynically: "we have herein no intention of diminishing your privileges, and we command that they continue and remain intact." Further quotation is superfluous.

All resistance was broken. Henri Sée made an analysis of the documents relating to the Angers revolt; they are of great significance in that the rebels in this town, which supposedly enjoyed the franchises of the La Rochelle commune, were notables. Louis XI kept a particularly close watch on Angers in that the town belonged, at least legally, to King René. He had installed as mayor one of his creatures, Guillaume de Cerisay, who filled the municipal offices with his relatives and friends. The wealthy burgesses complained bitterly, saying that the town hall was occupied by worthless people, "people of lowly condition", by "commoners and shoemakers". In 1478, when fresh elections were held, a score of notables stirred up a riot. Maître de Brye, who was sent by the king to restore order, had an escort of archers and an executioner. Twenty-six notables were arrested and tortured and some died in prison. The burgess body of Angers had to pay a fine of 12,000 *livres tournois*. For the rest of Louis' reign they dared not create a disturbance.

4. Urban oligarchies at the close of the Middle Ages

In order to obtain an accurate picture of the rise to power of oligarchies in the communes and *bonnes villes* in general at the close of the Middle Ages, we should need many local studies in depth and many histories of important burgess families. Such histories of towns as we have are nearly all superficial, and the archives of communes have provided numerous scholars with collections of tiny details from which no conclusions could be drawn. But there is enough documentary evidence to enable us to state that the tendency towards oligarchy was general. In the case of Amiens, which is typical, the process was demonstrated unequivocally. We have already seen that the offices of 'banner mayor' were annulled in 1382; from that date the craftsmen, now deprived of their leaders, exerted no further political influence. The general assemblies of inhabitants became increasingly the tool of plutocratic cliques. One or two families clung to power for an inordinate time. The Clabault family, for example, had acquired wealth in the cloth trade and were connected with some of the noble families of Picardy. Antoine Clabault, who seems to have been a rather remarkable man, was mayor fifteen times; he also held office for two five-year periods, the first from 1478 to 1483, the second from 1491 to 1496. In the century before, in a space of thirty-five years, Firmin Froiterie's name appears thirty-two times as an echevin and twice as a *compteur*. In the lists of thirty-nine successive bodies of echevins which ran from 1345 to 1382, there are only 131 different names. Between 1345 and 1503 the names of the burgesses who held office in Amiens numbered only 389.

It is not difficult to surmise the moral stature of the men who made up the urban oligarchies at the close of the Middle Ages. In Charles VII's reign, during the war against the English, men of ability with a gift for administration had been obliged to take over the running of public business, and the king had allowed them great freedom of action. But now the supreme virtues were docility and a servile obedience to the king's commands. Those who solicited municipal office were actuated solely by self-interest. They had been enticed by the king's flattery and his promises of benefits, and their sole ambition was to become ennobled, an ambition easily realized, which brought with it exemption from taxes and military service. The mayor of the Poitiers commune who, at the Estates-General of 1468 was known as 'first baron banneret' of the county of Poitou, must indeed have felt proud of his title. Men of independent character declined the office of mayor. There must have been many fathers who gave their sons the advice with which Etienne Benoît of Limoges prefaces his *Livre de raison* (in the words of his great uncle); "as regards civic affairs, get involved as little as possible".

Should we go further and believe that the town magistrates were swindlers? Louis XI must have often turned a blind eye to them; lack of integrity was not a serious vice, provided people 'toed the line'. In any case there are various pieces of evidence which lead one to suspect that there was corruption from one end of France to the other. Bernard Gros, the commander of the Temple at Breuil in the Agenais, wrote in 1480: "All the burgesses and others who govern the towns have grown rich, and at the present time several have seen that their grandfathers, or their fathers or themselves once possessed nothing, but now are rich and powerful. They are in league to consume and destroy the poor people and let everything fall to rack and ruin." They shifted their own taxes on to the poor, and they levied a larger tax than they were instructed to do, so as to make a profit for themselves, and they allowed no one from the humbler folk to assume office in the town, so that they could do just as they pleased.

At Limoges the sub-mayor, Lachosne Breton, who was appointed in 1476, made extortionate demands against which the inhabitants protested, but to no avail. In the territories of the duke of Burgundy there were the same complaints. In 1466 the duke introduced reforms into the Aire commune because the administration of justice and of the town's fairs, which was in the hands of a few families, was "carried on and maintained in an unsatisfactory manner". The inhabitants did not dare to lodge a complaint for fear of "greater hurt or harm". The same thing happened a few years earlier at Saint-Omer, where it had long been the practice for the two mayors and the echevins to distribute large sums of money to ensure their election; they committed endless abuses "not only in matters of justice and maintenance of law and order . . . but also as regards the bestowal of tax farms, assizes, and other rights belonging to this town". Saint-Omer sank more and more deeply into debt and lost many of its inhabitants, who preferred to go elsewhere. Though nepotism and extortion were not restricted to the royal domain or to Louis XI's reign, it must be observed that the despotism of the monarchy did not rid the communes and the other 'good towns' of these evils. And it served the king's purpose to see the cause of urban liberties with so few to champion it. The 'humble folk' were unlikely to mourn its decline, and commune franchises would disappear in a sea of indifference. Popular uprising would then be motivated only by the unfair distribution of taxes and the selfishness of the rich.

Index